THE CATHOLIC UNIVERSITY OF AMERICA
CANON LAW STUDIES
No. 125

THE MINISTER OF CONFIRMATION

AN HISTORICAL SYNOPSIS AND COMMENTARY

A DISSERTATION

Submitted to the Faculty of Canon Law of the Catholic University of America in Partial Fulfillment of the Requirements for the Degree of

DOCTOR OF CANON LAW

BY

REV. JOHN JEROME COLEMAN, J.C.L.
PRIEST OF THE DIOCESE OF SPOKANE

THE CATHOLIC UNIVERSITY OF AMERICA PRESS
WASHINGTON, D. C.
1941

NIHIL OBSTAT:

CLEMENT V. BASTNAGEL, J.U.D.
Censor Deputatus.

IMPRIMATUR:

✠ CAROLUS D. WHITE, D.D.,
Episcopus Spokanensis

Spokanensi die 17 Maii, 1941.

PRINTED IN THE UNITED STATES OF AMERICA
BY THE WATKINS PRINTING CO., BALTIMORE

TO THE HOLY GHOST
IN HUMBLE ACKNOWLEDGMENT
OF SPIRITUAL DIRECTION
AND MY FATHER AND MOTHER
IN TOKEN OF
FILIAL GRATITUDE

TABLE OF CONTENTS

PART ONE — HISTORICAL STUDY

PART TWO — CANONICAL COMMENTARY

Part One
HISTORICAL STUDY

INTRODUCTION

There is scarcely any ecclesiastic who will not commend a well-intentioned effort to expound and develop some phase of the doctrine and discipline of a Sacrament. But when a *canonical approach* is assumed in the treatment of a Sacrament, or of any other spiritual subject, it is likely to provoke an unfavorable reaction in some ecclesiastical minds, and to beget a suspicion that a sinister attempt is being made to deprive us of our heritage of freedom and to plunge us back into the "servitude of the law."[1]

This anti-canonical reaction is due to a lack of understanding of what a modern canonist calls "the connotative value" of the sacred canons.[2] The precepts of the Code are not just so many thou-shalts and thou-shalt-nots. This statement holds particularly with regard to the norms on the Minister of Confirmation. These norms reflect the Church's sympathetic understanding of her childrens' need of the strength and support that comes through the instrumentality of the Minister of Confirmation; they reflect the Church's special concern for the Catholics who are in danger of losing their faith, and their souls, in a hostile spiritual environment;[3] they reflect the orthodox sacramental doctrine in contradistinction to the errors of the "reformers" and the ante-Tridentine opinions of certain individual Catholics; they reflect the Church's desires and expectations regarding the Dispensers of the Mysteries of God.

With this understanding of the implications and the ulterior purposes of the legislation on the Ordinary and the Extraordinary Ministers of Confirmation the composition of this work has been undertaken. Given this assurance the reader has the right to expect (as the writer has the boldness to assume), that the fol-

[1] Cf. Romans, VII, 6.

[2] L. H. Motry, "The Connotative Value of the Sacred Canons," *The Jurist* (1941), 50-65.

[3] A source of canon 782, § 2; S. C. de Prop. Fide, Instr. 4 maii 1774—*Fontes,* n. 4565.

lowing pages will be of some benefit to the man whose interests are neither purely canonical nor purely academical.

On this occasion the writer wishes to thank his Bishop, the Most Reverend Charles D. White, D.D., for the opportunity of graduate work in Canon Law; he wishes to thank the individual members of the Faculty of Canon Law for their very helpful assistance; and he wishes to thank the librarians for services received.

PRELIMINARY OBSERVATIONS

There are some basic notions familiarity with which will be pre-supposed in the historical and explanatory divisions of this dissertation. These may be fittingly stated, or recalled, here as a sort of general introduction to the main theme.

Since the order of sanctifying grace is beyond the sphere of the natural man, the acquisition and increase of grace is dependent on the gratuitous disposition of Almighty God.[1] It is only He who can give sanctifying grace; and, unless He wishes to bestow it unconditionally and directly, it pertains to Him to determine the conditions or means whereby grace can be obtained and increased.[2]

Accordingly, the Divine Savior of the world has instituted specific signs or ceremonies called sacraments to be sources or channels of grace,[3] and upon the performance of these signs, ceremonies or actions in the proper circumstances by the competent minister sanctifying grace is conveyed to the soul.[4]

From this one can understand what is meant by the term, "minister of a sacrament." It is the person who performs the sacramental action in the name of Christ.[5] Because the action derives its efficacy from its Author and Principal Minister, Jesus Christ, the human minister is said to operate *in the name of Christ.*[6]

By divine institution there are *consecrated* and *non-consecrated* ministers. Consecrated ministers are those who obtain their competence from a special consecration.[7] They are required for the

[1] Cf. Tanquerey, *Synopsis Theologiae Dogmaticae* (3 vols., Vols. I, II, 24. ed., Vol. III, 23. ed., Parisiis: Desclee et Socii, 1934-1937), III, n. 7.

[2] Cf. Tanquerey, *op. cit.,* III, n. 292.

[3] Conc. Trident., Sess. VI, *de ref.,* c. 1.

[4] Cf. Tanquerey, *op. cit.,* III, n. 405; Conc. Trident., Sess. VI, cc. 6, 7.

[5] Cf. Noldin-Schmitt, *Summa Theologiae Moralis* (3 vols., 20. ed., Ratisbonae: Pustet, 1929), III, n. 17.

[6] Cf. Noldin-Schmitt, *loc. cit.*

[7] Cf. Cappello, *De Sacramentis* (3 vols., Vols. I-II, 3. ed., Taurinorum Augustae: Marietti, 1938; Vol. III, 4. ed., Taurinorum Augustae: Marietti, 1939), I, n. 40.

valid administration [8] of all the sacraments except baptism and matrimony. Non-consecrated ministers are those who are, as it were, naturally competent without a special consecration. They can confer only the sacraments of baptism and matrimony.

With regard to baptism and confirmation, there is the further division of minister into *ordinary* and *extraordinary.* In the case of baptism a priest is the ordinary [9] and a deacon the extraordinary minister.[10] Here the reason for the distinction seems to be that, in ordinary circumstances or without a "just cause," a deacon cannot lawfully baptize,[11] whereas this limitation is not placed upon a priest. The basis for the distinction regarding the foregoing ministers of baptism seems to have its roots in ecclesiastical law only.

In reference to confirmation the ordinary minister is he who *by virtue of his ordination alone* has the power to confirm validly.[12] Thus the bishop by reason of his episcopal consecration is the ordinary minister of confirmation. The extraordinary minister of confirmation is he who in virtue of his ordination *plus a special commission from the Pope* is capable of administering confirmation.[13] It is very probable, if not altogether certain, that by *divine law* a simple priest without papal delegation is incapable of confirming,[14] while episcopal consecration gives an irrevocable power to confirm.[15]

The diversity of legislation which obtains regarding Greek and Latin ministers, as well as Greek and Latin subjects, of confirmation[16] makes it necessary for the canonist to be able to distin-

[8] "Administration" must be understood in the sense of *confection* in the case of the Blessed Eucharist, for this sacrament exists independently of its administration.

[9] Canon 738.

[10] Canon 741.

[11] Cf. Canon 741.

[12] Cf. Blat, *Commentarium Textus Codicis Iuris Canonici* (6 vols., Romae: Collegio Angelico, 1921-1927), III, Pars I, n. 76.

[13] Cf. Blat, *loc. cit.*

[14] Cf. p.

[15] Cf. Chap. III, Art. 2.

[16] Canon 782, §§ 4, 5.

guish between the two main divisions of the one Catholic Church.

"The expression 'Latin Church' indicates not only the Roman Rite, but all rites pertaining to the Latin Church, such as the Ambrosian Rite of Milan, Italy, the Lyonese Rite (Gallican) in France, and the Mozarabic Rite used in Toledo, Spain, including also rites of certain religious orders (Dominicans, Carthusians, Carmelites)."[17]

"The Oriental Church comprises those churches (rites) which are, or have been, subject to the jurisdiction of the Oriental Patriarchs.[18] As their main rites these churches employ the Byzantine, Alexandrine, Antiochene, Armenian, and Chaldean, and of these main rites many varieties are in use.[19]

The Code determines how a person becomes subject to the Latin or to a Greek rite. It states: "A person belongs to that rite by the ceremonies of which he was baptized, unless (1) the baptism was administered by a priest of another rite who had no authority to baptize but did so fraudently, or who baptized in case of necessity, when no priest of the proper rite could be secured; or (2) by apostolic indult a person obtained permission to be baptized with the ceremonies of a certain rite without the obligation of adhering to that rite."[20] A woman who belongs to a rite different from that of her prospective husband may at the time of the marriage, or any time during the marriage, join the rite of her husband. After the marriage has been dissolved she may generally return to her former rite.[21] In other cases the permission of the Holy See is necessary to permit one's transition from an Oriental rite to the Latin rite, or *vice versa.*

These introductory observations may furnish a basis for a more

[17] Cicognani, *Canon Law* (2. English ed., Philadelphia: The Dolphin Press, 1935), p. 444.

[18] Vermeersch-Creusen, *Epitome Iuris Canonici* (3 vols., Vol. I, 6. ed., Vols. II-III, 5. ed., Mechliniae: Dessain, 1934-1937), I, n. 67.

[19] Cf. Attwater, *The Catholic Eastern Church* (2. ed., Milwaukee: Bruce, 1937), pp. 41 ff.

[20] Canon 98, § 1.

[21] Canon 98, § 4.

[22] Canon 98, § 3.

comprehensive grasp of the terms *ordinary* and *extraordinary* ministers as employed in subsequent pages; they may also enable the reader to obtain a clearer understanding of the legislation founded on a diversity of rite.

Chapter I

THE ORDINARY AND EXTRAORDINARY MINISTERS OF CONFIRMATION

Article 1. The Ordinary Minister

The Code of Canon Law merely restates a defined doctrine,[1] when it says that the bishop alone is the ordinary minister of confirmation.[2] The law, however, invites historical study, not only because conflicting views have been held regarding the minister of confirmation,[3] but also because a full appreciation of the respective positions of the bishop-minister and the priest-minister can come only from an historical examination of the Church's legislation and practice with regard to those functionaries.

In the New Testament there are probably but two certain references to the actual administration of the sacrament of confirmation.[4] In the Acts of the Apostles, VIII, 1, there is mention of a persecution of Christians in Jerusalem which caused them to be dispersed throughout Judea and Samaria. Philip, the deacon, went to the city of Samaria, and by his teaching and miracles won over a large number of converts to the new faith and baptized them. At this point the Acts go on to say:

> "Now when the apostles, who were at Jerusalem had heard that Samaria had received the word of God; they sent unto them Peter and John. Who when they were

[1] *"Si quis dixerit sanctae confirmationis ordinarium ministrum non esse solum episcopum, sed quemvis simplicem sacerdotem, anathema sit."* —Conc. Trident., sess. VII, *de confirmatione*, can. 3.

[2] Canon 782, § 1.

[3] Cf. Cappello, *Tractatus Canonico-Moralis de Sacramentis* (3 vols., Vol. I, II, 3. ed., Taurinorum Augustae: Marietti, 1939, Vol. III, 4. ed., Taurinorum Augustae: Marietti, 1939), I, n. 204; O'Dwyre, *Confirmation* (New York, 1915), p. 162 ff.; Photius, *Ep. XIII*, §§ 6, 7—*MPG*, CII, 725. Subsequently the preceding work of Cappello will be designated: "De Sacramentis."

[4] Cf. D'Ales, *De Baptismo et Confirmatione* (Parisiis: Beauchesne, 1927), p. 168.

> come prayed for them that they might receive the Holy Ghost; for he was not yet come upon them; but they were only baptized in the name of the Lord Jesus. Then they laid their hands upon them and they received the Holy Ghost."[5]

The other undisputed instance of the administration of confimation in the New Testament is in the Acts, XIX, 1-6. It reads:

> "And it came to pass while Apollo was at Corinth, that Paul having passed through the upper coasts, came to Ephesus and found certain disciples: and he said to them, have you received the Holy Ghost since ye believed? But they said to him: We have not so much as heard if there be a Holy Ghost. And he said: In what then were you baptized? Who said: In John's baptism. Then Paul said: John baptized the people with the baptism of penance saying: that they should believe in him who was to come after him, that is in Jesus. Having heard these things they were baptized in the name of the Lord Jesus. And when Paul had imposed his hands upon them the Holy Ghost came upon them, and they spoke with tongues and prophesied."

Taking these passages in themselves, without regard for their traditional interpretation, one can scarcely accept them as conclusive proof of any special reservation to the bishop of the administration of confirmation.[6] It is not stated even implicitly in the Acts, or elsewhere in the New Testament, that on their visit to Samaria Peter and John acted as bishops and not simply as priests. Nor is there any indication that there were yet simple priests in the Church who, in any hypothesis, could have gone to Samaria instead of the apostles. Conceding on the other hand that there were simple priests enjoying a part in the ecclesiastical ministry, when Paul reached Ephesus on his second missionary journey,[7] that does not prove that St. Paul administered con-

[5] Acts, VIII, 14.

[6] Cf. O'Dwyre, *Confirmation*, p. 166.

[7] Cf. Tournely, *Tractatus de Universa Theologia Morali* (8 vols., Parisiis, 1750), VIII, 135. Afterwards the title, *"Theologia Moralis,"* will be used to refer to this work of Tournely.

firmation to the Ephesians, simply because its administration was understood to be ordinarily the work of those in episcopal orders.

But while, at least to the average reader, these passages from the Acts do not seem to be of themselves decisive or even probative, it is a noteworthy and significant fact that leading authorities, including some of the most distinguished pontiffs, have appealed to them in order to vindicate the bishop's special prerogative as a minister of confirmation.[8] The Acts have been so interpreted in papal documents of unusual importance.[9] Whatever, therefore, the texts in question may mean to the casual reader, it is certain that according to traditional and authoritative interpretations they have been understood to prove a peculiar, episcopal right and faculty in the administration of confirmation.

Apart from the passages cited from the Acts, the references to confirmation during the first two centuries of Christianity are very rare, and the references available on that period are very obscure,[10] though of course that does not imply that confirmation was not generally being administered. Baptism and confirmation were usually administered together as the Christian Initiation Rite,[11] and hence there was little occasion to distinguish one sacrament from the other.

However, the early reservation of the administration of baptism

[8] Cf. Cyprian, *Ep. LXXII—MPL,* III, 1160; Augustine, *De Trinitate,* Cap. XXVI—*MPL,* XLII, 1003; Chrysostom, *Hom. XVIII* in cap. VIII, Act. Apost.—*MPG,* CLX, 144; Isidore of Seville, *De Officiis Ecclesiasticis —MPL,* LXXXIII, 820; Innocent I, *Ep. ad Decentium—MPL,* XX, 554; c. un., X, *de sacra unctione,* I, 15; Innocent IV—*Fontes,* n. 34, § 3; Eugene IV, *Exultate Deo*—Denzinger-Umberg, *Enchiridion Symbolorum Definitonum et Declarationum,* ed. 21-23, Friburgi Brisgoviae: Herder, 1937, n. 697.

[9] Cf. papal documents mentioned in the preceding footnote, especially that of Eugene IV.

[10] Cf. O'Dwyre, *Confirmation,* p. 21; D'Ales, *De Baptismo et Confirmatione,* p. 172.

[11] "Exinde egressi de lavacro, perungimur benedicta unctione. Dehinc manus imponitur per benedictionem advocans et invitans Spiritum Sanctum." Tertullian, *Lib. de Bap.,* cap. 8, § 8—*MPL,* I, 1206; cf. Chardon, *Histoire des Sacramens* (6 vols., Parisiis, 1745), I, 327.

to the bishop,[12] implied also the reservation of the administration of confirmation to him, for the latter solemn ceremony which constituted the perfect Christian would have been more appropriately performed by a bishop than by a simple priest.[13] Yet the temporary reservation to the bishop of the right to baptize was not at any time taken as the reason for the reservation of confirmation to him, for it will be seen that, when in some emergency a priest was permitted to baptize, the persons so baptized had afterwards to be taken to the bishop for confirmation.[14] From the third century on there is positive clear evidence of the bishop's peculiar right.

About the year 250 occurs a reference made by a Pope to the bishop as the one accepted minister of confirmation. In a letter to Fabius, Bishop of Antioch, Cornelius writes of an unworthy priest called Novation: "Moreover, when he recovered from his illness, he never observed the other things which a man ought to observe according to the ecclesiastical rule: neither was he sealed by a bishop. But not having received the seal in any way, how then could he have obtained the Holy Ghost?" [15] Thus in one of the earliest references to the minister of confirmation after apostolic times, a pope assumes that the bishop, and at least in the ordinary course no one else, administers the sacrament of confirmation.[16] Though the reference Cornelius makes to the minister is only casual, it is evidently very significant in so far as it gives the recognized practice.

About the same time there appears the very explicit testimony of St. Cyprian of Carthage, and notwithstanding his error on the baptismal question, the testimony which the great Metropolitan of Carthage offers on the minister of confirmation is obviously of particular importance. Referring to the imposition of hands made on the Samaritans by the apostles Cyprian writes:

[12] Cf. Tertullian, *Lib. de Bap.*, Cap. XVII—*MPL*, I, 1218; St. Jerome, *Dialog. adversus Luciferanos*—*MPL*, XXIII, 164.

[13] Cf. St. Thomas, *Summa Theologica*, q. LXXVII, art. 11.

[14] Cf. Concilium Eliberitanum, can. 77—Harduin, I, 256

[15] *MPL*, XX, 623.

[16] Cf. *Dictionaire de Théologie Catholique, s.v. "Confirmation."*

> "Which [16a] thing takes place now amongst us also, namely, those who are baptized in the Church are presented to the rulers of the Church that through our prayer and the imposition of hands they may receive the Holy Ghost and be made perfect with the seal of the Lord." [17]

There can be no question but the rulers of the Church, or the *praepositi Ecclesiae,* were bishops.[18] Furthermore he says: "by *our* prayer and the imposition of hands," words which indicate the ceremony was performed by himself and by others, *like the bishop he was addressing,* of the same rank: in all cases therefore by bishops. Even the comparison he makes between the apostles and *the rulers of the Church* in his day seems to indicate that to his mind the administration of confirmation belonged properly to those who succeeded the apostles in the hierarchy of orders.

As early as the year 350 we have the authority of an important council in favor of the point that is here maintained. Canon 38 of the Council of Elvira directs what is to be done, when a lay person administers baptism in an emergency:

> "In making a sea voyage to a foreign place or in the instance where a church is not within easy reach, one of the faithful who has kept himself pure and has not been twice married may baptize a catechumen who has fallen into serious illness, but on the condition that, if the person recover, he be *brought to the bishop to be made perfect by the imposition of hands.*" [19]

This bringing of the baptized person to the bishop to have him made perfect refers, in the language of the times, to the administration of confirmation.[20] There is no hint that one who has been baptized in a serious illness by an ordinary Christian could

[16a] All translations whose authorship is not specifically indicated are the work of the writer.

[17] *Ep. LXXIII, ad Jubaianum—MPL,* III, 1160.

[18] Cf. Deslandes, "Le Pretre Oriental Ministre de la Confirmation," *Echos D'Orient,* XXIX (1930), 6.

[19] Harduin, I, 254.

[20] Cf. Cyril of Alexandria on John VII—*MPG,* LXXIV, 49; Dionysius Areopagita, *De Ecc. Hier.—MPG,* III, 404.

in any circumstances be brought to a priest for confirmation. That shows that in the judgment of the Fathers of this council there was no occasion, or practically no occasion, in which a priest could confirm. In other words, the council believed confirmation to be reserved in a very strict manner to bishops.[21]

Canon 77 of the same council has this direction for deacons: "If a deacon who has charge of a community baptize some people in the absence of priest or bishop, the bishop must perfect them by his blessing." [22] The terminology of this canon, like that of the preceding designates the ceremony of confirmation.

Its exact interpretation however has presented some difficulty. It has even been given as an objection that priests at that time commonly administered the sacrament of confirmation.[23]

In answer to that objection it may easily be said that the council does not say anything, nor does it necessarily imply anything, regarding those who have been baptized by a priest. Besides, if a priest were understood to administer confirmation regularly, it is not apparent why the council orders those baptized by a deacon to be brought to a bishop for confirmation, there being no indication that such people might go to a priest, though priests were undoubtedly more numerous and therefore more accessible at that time.[24] Even at first sight the canon seems to be in favor of the exclusive, or practically exclusive, right of the bishop.

But why the strange wording of the canon? May it not be that the council did not regard the priest or deacon as having the right to baptize in the ordinary course? [25] It would seem then that

[21] Cf. D'Ales, *De Baptismo et Confirmatione*, p. 158; Diekamp, *Theologiae Dogmaticae Manuale* (2 vols., 7. ed., Parisiis: Desclee et Sociorum, 1933).

[22] Harduin, I, 258.

[23] Cf. Tournelly, *Theologia Moralis*, VIII, 139.

[24] Cf. Poulet-Raemers, *Church History* (2 vols., 2. English ed., London: Herder, 1936), I, 256.

[25] Tertullian writes thus: "*Dandi quidem (baptismi) habet jus summus sacerdos, qui est episcopus. Dehinc presbyteri et diaconi, non tamen sine episcopi auctoritate.*" *Lib. de Bap.*, Cap. XVII—*MPL,* I, 1218; Jerome likewise says: "*Sine . . . episcopi jussione nec presyter nec diaconus jus habet baptizandi.*" *Dialog. adversus Luciferanos—MPL,*

when the priest did baptize it was in some emergency; perhaps it was only in danger of death, or in some other very urgent circumstances. In such circumstances, in view of the wording of the canon, it appears quite probable that he also confirmed. This interpretation of canon 77 is supported by a number of canons that will be cited in the next article to show that not so very long after the Council of Elvira priests in France and Spain had the right to administer confirmation to dying heretics. Taken in this way, the canon fits in with the general legislation of the period, and is a good argument that the Fathers of Elvira looked to the bishop as the usual minister of confirmation. It may be observed, finally, that both canons are amongst the classic texts used to show the bishop's peculiar right regarding the administration of confirmation.[26]

St. Jerome makes a statement that is here very much to the point: "I do not deny that it is the custom of the churches that the bishop goes out to impose hands on those who, at a distance in the smaller towns, have been baptized by priests or deacons." [27] Here Jerome gives *the custom of the churches,* and says in accordance with that custom the bishop *went out to the outlying small towns and communities* to administer confirmation to people previously baptized by a priest or deacon. Though these journeys must have caused the bishop considerable hardship and inconvenience, he was obliged to go personally and administer confirmation in the remote parts of his diocese. Not even to save the bishop a great amount of labor and loss of time entailed in long wearisome journeys, could a priest be legitimately authorized to administer confirmation. With so much strictness was confirmation reserved to the bishop according to the custom given by Jerome.[28]

On the minister of confirmation there is an important and frequently quoted letter by Pope Innocent I (401-417) to bishop Decentius of the diocese of Gubbio. In this letter the Pontiff writes:

XXIII, 164; cf. also Martene, *De Antiquis Ecclesiae Ritibus* (3 vols., Rotomagi, 1700), I, cap. 1, art. 3.

[26] Cf. *Dictionaire de Theologie Catholique,* s.v. "Confirmation."

[27] *MPL,* XXIII, 164.

[28] Cf. Van Noort, *De Sacramentis* (2. ed., Amstelodami, 1910), p. 210.

> "With regard to the confirmation of infants, it is manifest that it should not be done by anyone but by the bishop. For presbyters, though they are priests, have not the dignity of the episcopal office: and that it is the prerogative of the bishop alone to mark with chrism is evident not only from the custom of the churches, but likewise from the reading of the very Acts of the Apostles, which relate that Peter and John were sent to communicate the Holy Ghost to those who had already been baptized. For priests baptizing either in the absence or presence of the bishop are allowed to anoint with chrism those whom they baptize, provided it be consecrated by the bishop: *but not to mark the forehead with the same oil which is the privilege of the bishops alone, when they communicate the Holy Ghost.*"[29]

In the arguments cited prior to this letter of Innocent I the references to the bishop as being in a peculiar manner the minister of confirmation were purely casual, though sufficiently cogent. Innocent on the other hand is dealing with the subject of the minister *ex professo,* and he is speaking with the authority which attaches to the successor of Peter. The style of his letter moreover is so explicit and emphatic that it leaves nothing to mere inference. Note the force of his words: It is *manifest* that confirmation should not be administered by anyone except by bishops. Priests may not administer it, for the simple reason that they are only priests and not bishops. Then the custom of the churches—a telling argument in early Christian times—is appealed to as proof to the exclusive prerogative of the bishop. Lastly, the Pope refers to the Acts of the Apostles as the final argument that it is the peculiar right of the bishop to confirm. In the Acts it was deemed necessary to send two bishops, Peter and John, down from Jerusalem to Samaria to confirm the Samaritan converts; and that very fact, according to the reasoning of Innocent, demonstrates the necessity for the special reservation of confirmation to bishops at all times. It is scarcely possible, then, to have stronger support than this letter of Innocent I for the position defended in this chapter.[30]

[29] *MPL,* XX, 555.

[30] Cf. Deslandes, "Le Pretre Oriental Ministre de la Confirmation,"

Later in the same century Pope Gelasius not only speaks emphatically about the bishop's peculiar right to confirm, but he looks on the bishop's right as such an accepted and unquestionable fact that he assumes a tone of stern rebuke in condemning a particular contrary practice. He charges the bishops of Lucania (Sicily) in this manner:

"We forbid priests to attempt to go beyond their own sphere brazenly presuming to have for themselves what belongs to the episcopal dignity, blessing chrism, and seizing for themselves the pontifical prerogative of sealing."[31] This order of Gelasius needs no comment, for the very tone of his letter implies that he regarded the priests of Lucania as guilty of a very serious abuse, when they presumed to administer confirmation.[32]

The next case deserving of special consideration is, that of Gregory I and the priests of the diocese of Cagliari (Sardinia). The Pope heard that priests were confirming in this diocese. Therefore he wrote to Januarius, their bishop, as follows:

"Priests are not to presume to sign baptized infants on the forehead with the sacred chrism; but priests may administer it on the breast, that bishops may afterwards administer it on the forehead."[33]

It must be maintained, the contrary opinion of Saintebeauve and others notwithstanding,[34] that there is reference to confirmation in Gregory's letter.[35] If the sealing of a person on the forehead were a mere ceremony or sacramental, there would be no reason for its being reserved so strictly to the bishop, or for the Pope's directing priests not to *presume* to administer it.[36]

Echos D'Orient, XXIX (1930), 6; Souarn, "De Presbytero Orientali Confirmationis Ministro," *Jus Pontificium,* XI (1931), 134; Tournely, *Theologia Moralis,* VIII, 301.

[31] *MPL, XLIX,* 50.

[32] Cf. Souarn, *loc. cit.*

[33] *Ep. IX—MPL,* LXXVII, 677.

[34] Cf. *Tractatus de Sacramento Confirmationis* (Lovanii, 1778), 450.

[35] Lahouse, *Universa Theologia Scholastica* (2 vols., Brugis, 1904), II, 376 ff.

[36] Cf. Benedict XIV, *De Synodo Diocesana,* Vol. II, cap. 7, n. 5.

Assuming, then, that Gregory is speaking of confirmation, it should be noted how very emphatic he is in this prohibition. He uses the word, presume, which indicates an unwarranted and altogether irregular assumption of power on the part of the priests of Cagliari. He does not indeed say that these priests were acting invalidly. But that does not imply that he considered their action valid. Expedience might well have counselled, first, that re-confirmation should not be insisted on, and, secondly, that nothing should be said regarding validity or invalidity. It is known that Gregory in his relations with these people, while endeavoring to remove abuses, was very careful not to give unnecessary occasion for scandal or disquietude.[37] According to such a policy, Gregory might well have been persuaded that he should not insist on re-confirmation.

Now the importance of the Pontiff's letter is more apparent, when it is remembered that in forbidding the priests of Cagliari to confirm he claims to have been acting in accordance with the ancient usage of the Roman Church: that is, with the Church which is the criterion of orthodox teaching and practice.[38]

If Gregory modified his ruling the following year, it was because he was, as it were, compelled to do so. It was, as he himself asserts, because certain people, presumably a large number of people were scandalized by the rigor of his first letter.[39] The first letter of Gregory is strongly in favor of the peculiar prerogative of the bishop. The second letter may be said to be as much in favor of the same position, for as an express exception it is indicative of the rule.

After Gregory's time there are some particular councils which it seems of advantage to cite on the minister of confirmation. A council of Seville in the year 619 rules: "It is not lawful for

[37] Cf. *Ep. XXVII—MPL,* LXXVII, 696.

[38] *Ep. XXVI*: " . . . Et nos quidem secundum usum veterum Ecclesiae Nostrae fecimus."—*MPL,* LXXVII, 696.

[39] "Pervenit quoque ad nos quosdam scandalizatos fuisse, . . . sed si omnino hac de re aliqui contristantur, ubi episcopi desunt, ut presbyteri etiam in frontibus baptizatos tangere debeant concedimus." *ibi.;* cf. also a note by Gratian, c. 2, D. XCV.

priests by imposing hands to impart the Holy Ghost to baptized members of the faithful, or to converts from heresy, . . . because they have not the perfection of the episcopate . . . . "[40] The scholarly Isidore of Seville, who was present at the council, may be cited by way of commentary on this canon. He says that the baptism of the Holy Ghost is given by bishops with imposition of hands. Then he refers to Acts XIX and to Innocent I as proof that it is the peculiar right of the bishop to impose hands.[41]

In Germany a council at Ratisbon (742) admonishes pastors to be prepared to receive the bishop when he goes around the diocese to administer confirmation, thus assuming that it is the bishop who always does that.[42] Another council at Worms (862) says explicitly that priests must not confirm: " . . . it is not lawful for priests to give the Paraclete Spirit by imposing hands, . . . for all these things are understood to be unlawful for priests because they have not the dignity of bishops." [43]

The pontifical letters of the succeeding centuries, like those already cited, are all alike in their strong emphasis on the peculiar right of the bishop. For the sake of brevity, and because of their similarity, these letters will be considered together. They will not need much comment.

Nicholas I (858-867) not only stressed the bishop's peculiar right as a minister of confirmation, but he went so far as to order a re-confirmation of Bulgarians who had been confirmed by priests delegated by Photius of Constantinople.[44]

In 1199 Innocent III wrote to his representative at Constantinople:

> "It has come to our knowledge that certain priests at Constantinople have presumed to administer to the faith-

[40] Canon 7—Harduin, III, 560.

[41] *De Officiis Ecclesiasticis—MPL,* LXXXIII, 820.

[42] Cap. III—Harduin, III, 1920.

[43] Canon 8—Mansi, XV, 871; cf. also Council of Paris (829), Lib. I, cap. 27—Mansi, XIV, 556.

[44] *MPL,* CXIX, 921; cf. Souarn, "De Presbytero Orientali Confirmationis Ministro," *Jus Pontificium,* XI (1931), 141 ff.

ful those sacraments which from the time of the apostles have been reserved to the bishop, as is the sacrament of confirmation, . . . We ask you (as our representative) strictly to forbid this, lest priests should rashly presume to do this in the future."[45]

In 1204 the same Pope wrote to Bulgaria:

"While a simple priest can give the other unctions, only a bishop can administer this (confirmation), for it is only of the Apostles whose successors are the bishops that it is read: 'They gave the Holy Ghost by imposition of hands'." [46]

Innocent IV uses almost the same language writing in 1254:

"Only the bishop may sign baptized people with chrism on the forehead, for we read that it was only the apostles, whose place the bishops have taken, who gave the Holy Spirit." [47] It will be noted that these popes are as strict and insistent with regard to the reservation of confirmation to the bishop as were Innocent I and Gelasius I,[48] and they too appeal to the acts of the apostles as the reason for the reservation.

The Scholastic Theologians were all agreed on the bishop's right and faculty in reference to confirmation.[49] So much indeed was the bishop's prerogative emphasized that some of the leading scholastics denied that a simple priest could be delegated to confirm in any circumstances.[50]

The Council of Florence (1438-1445) in a very important document used the words, *ordinary minister,* to indicate the bishop's prerogative regarding confirmation. This council which sought to affect a reunion of the Greeks and Latins issued (1439) a famous decree or instruction in which many points of Catholic

[45] C. 4, X, *de consuetudine,* I, 4; This command is understood to have affected only the Latin priests in Constantinople; cf. Holtzclan, *Theologia Dogmatica* (3 vols., 3. ed., Parisiis, 1880), III, 277.

[46] C. un., X, *de sacra unctione,* I, 15.

[47] *Fontes,* n. 34, § 3.

[48] Cf. *MPL,* XX, 555; LXXVII, 677.

[49] Cf. O'Dwyre, *Confirmation,* p. 162.

[50] Cf. Albert the Great, *Commentarii in IV Sententiarum,* Dist. VII, Art. IV; Durandus, *In Petri Lombardi Sententias Theologicas,* Lib. IV, Dist. VII.

doctrine were defined for the Armenians and Jacobites. With reference to confirmation the Decree said:

> "The second sacrament is confirmation . . . The ordinary minister of this sacrament is the bishop; and though the other unctions may be given by a simple priest, only the bishop ought to perform this one; for it is only of the apostles whose place the bishops have taken that we read: 'They gave the Holy Ghost by imposition of hands' We may read however that a simple priest has for a reasonable and urgent cause been delegated by the Apostolic See to give confirmation."[51]

This Decree stated only what in the West had long been the accepted doctrine on the bishop; but it was probably a revelation for some of the Orientals who had been accustomed to seeing confirmation regularly administered by priests.[52] It was thought by some however that the Council of Florence did not settle the question as to whether or not the bishop was the one, exclusive minister of confirmation.[53] It has been seen that some of the scholastics maintained that he was.[54]

When the subject of the minister of confirmation came up at the Council of Trent, the Fathers desired only to condemn the erroneous teaching of the reformers. For this purpose they issued the following canon: "If anyone says that the bishop is not the sole ordinary minister of confirmation let him be anathema."[55] It thus became an article of faith that the bishop is the sole ordinary minister of confirmation; though even yet some held that it was not authoritatively settled whether there might not in some circumstances be a priest-minister.

From the foregoing pages it cannot be inferred that the bishop was always recognized as the ordinary minister of confirmation in the modern accepted sense of the term. Still it is clear that from the beginning he was regarded by the Church itself as hav-

[51] Denzinger, *Enchiridion*, n. 697.
[52] Cf. *infra*, Art. 3.
[53] Cf. O'Dwyre, *Confirmation*, p. 164.
[54] Cf. *infra*, footnote 81.
[55] Sess. VII, *de confirmatione*, can. 3.

ing a special and peculiar prerogative as a minister of confirmation. Even before the Council of Trent the bishop's position was outside the realm of discussion. Now it cannot be questioned. His position however as ordinary minister of confirmation will be clearer and more defined after the extraordinary minister has been subjected to historical study.

Article 2. The Extraordinary Minister

It is difficult to determine when the faculty to confirm was first given to simple priests. The earliest alleged instances of their confirming are not unanimously accepted by students.[56] Consequently a case about which there is practically complete agreement does not occur before the end of the sixth century.[57]

One of the earliest quoted witnesses on the priest-minister is St. Jerome. In an epistle against Evagrius Jerome asks: "Except ordaining, what does a bishop do that a priest does not also do?" [58] While it is certain that Jerome did not regard the priest as the usual minister of confirmation,[59] his question here supposes that he regards the priest as having in some cases the faculty to confirm, or at least as capable of receiving such a faculty. And that was Jerome's conviction, when baptism itself was ordinarily reserved to bishops,[60] and when they were accustomed to visit the remote parts of their diocese for the purpose of administering confirmation.[61] Thus one of our earliest witnesses on the priest-minister seems to be in complete agreement with the modern orthodox teaching.[62]

A series of councils in the fifth and sixth centuries is frequently quoted to show that the priest was in certain contingencies authorized to administer confirmation. About 401 the Council of

[56] Cf. Benedict XIV, *De Synodo Dioecesana,* Lib. VII, cap. 8, nn. 5-6.

[57] Gregory I, *Ep. XXVI—MPL,* LXXVII, 696.

[58] *MPL,* XXII, 1194.

[59] Cf. *Dialog. adversus Luciferanos—MPL,* XXIII, 164.

[60] Cf. Tertullian, *Lib. de Bap.—MPL,* I, 1218.

[61] Cf. St. Jerome, *Dialog. adversus Luciferanos—MPL,* XXIII, 164.

[62] Important fourth century evidence regarding priests confirming in Alexandria and Egypt is found in the next article.

Toledo made this regulation:"It has been defined that a priest but not a deacon may administer chrism, when the bishop is absent, and even when the bishop is present, if the bishop commands him to do so." [63] In this instance the use of chrism is of course taken for the administration of the sacrament of confirmation.[64] That the reference was to confirmation seems to be indirectly proved by a letter of Innocent I dating from about this time.[65] He recognized the priest's right to administer chrism as a sacramental, whether the bishop happened to be present or not. The Council of Toledo on the other hand makes reference to a use of chrism which is permitted to priests, only in the absence of a bishop, or, if a bishop is present, only with an express order from him. It can hardly therefore be speaking of a mere sacramental, but must be conceding to priests the faculty to administer confirmation.[66]

The Council of Orange (441) and the Council of Arles (452) have almost identical canons on the reception of heretics in danger of death. The Fathers of Orange decreed: "If heretics who are in danger of death desire to be Catholics, and a bishop is not available, the sealing with chrism and benediction should be made by priests.[67] Because of a similar ruling made by the Council of Epaon in the following century (517) that council will be cited here, and then the legislation of the three councils may be simultaneously discussed, and interpreted. The law made by the Councils of Epaon was thus formulated:

> "For the sake of the salvation of souls, which we desire in all cases, we give priests permission to succor by an unction

[63] Canon 20—Harduin, I, 992.

[64] Cf. Zerba, "Instructio pro Simplice Sacerdote Sacramentum Confirmationis ex Sedis Apostolicae Delegatione Administranti," *Apollinaris,* VIII (1935), 41.

[65] *MPL,* XX, 555.

[66] Cf. Benedict XIV, *De Synodo Dioecesana,* Lib. VII, cap. 7, n. 5.

[67] Canon 1: "Haereticos in mortis discrimine positos, si catholici esse desiderant, si desit episcopus, a presbyteris cum chrismate et benedictione consignari placuit."—Mansi, VI, 435; canon 26 of the Council of Arles differs only in this that it has *chrismatis benedictione* instead of *chrismate et benedictione.*

with chrism those ill, despairing heretics who desire an immediate conversion. But others who while in good health seek to be converted must understand that they shall have to wait for the bishop."[68]

While admitting that canon 1 of the council of Toledo refers to confirmation, Bareille dismisses these canons with the comment that there is question of a mere reconciliation ceremony.[69] Benedict XIV concedes that these canons probably do refer to confirmation, and that perhaps they give priests the faculty to administer it; yet he seems to favor the view that the councils have only a reconciliation in mind.[70] But without any distortion of the canons it does seem probable that they have to do with confirmation. The rite here prescribed is very similar to the rite which the I General Council of Constantinople (381) laid down for the reception of heretics,[71] and which Benedict himself admits to be confirmation.[72] In the anointing ordered by the Council of Constantinople the words *donum Spiritus Sancti* were to be pronounced by the person doing the anointing. But while there is no reference to the Holy Ghost in the canons under discussion, a sacrament does seem to be implied in them. The words, benediction and chrism, or benediction of chrism, are not much unlike the phrase used by the Council of Elvira to designate the sacrament of confirmation.[73] The Council of Epaon says that it is *for the sake of the salvation of souls* that it is disposed to make this special concession to priests on behalf of sick, despairing heretics who want to be converted. Here is an implication that the cere-

[68] Canon 16—Harduim, II, 1049.

[69] *Dictionnaire de Theologie Catholique,* s.v. "Confirmation."

[70] *De Synodo Dioecesana,* lib. VII, cap. 8.

[71] Canon 7: " . . . *Arianos . . . recipimus dantes quidem libellos, et omnem haeresim anathematizantes, quae non sentit ut facta Dei Catholica et Apostolica Ecclesia, signatos sive unctos primum sancto chrismate, et frontem et oculos et nares et os et aures et eos signantes dicimus 'Signaculum Doni Spiritus Sancti'* ".—Mansi, III, 653.

[72] Monita on New Edition of Euchologium—*Bullarium Sacrae Congregationis de Propaganda Fide,* III, 425.

[73] Canon 77—Harduin, I, 258.

mony is directly and immediately connected with the salvation of souls. Hence it is more probable that it is a sacrament than a mere reconciliation rite. No one of course would question the paramount importance, if not moral necessity, of confirmation to heretics who feel that they are about to be called to answer for their stewardship. The learned De Petra understands these canons as referring to confirmation. He says: "The permission of a synod was necessary to allow priests to make the blessing in this case, because in the ordinary course this ministry belongs to the bishops, as Innocent I testified."[74]

There is certainly nothing inherently improbable in the view that there is reference to confirmation; because though the rule of Innocent I and of Gelasius I very strictly reserved confirmation to bishops, it could be maintained that these popes were providing for the average case, and did not contemplate cases of real, urgent necessity. If it be granted that there is reference to confirmation, then note must be taken of the fact that it was only for cases of real, urgent necessity that the faculty to confirm was given to a priest by these councils. At most he was considered only an emergency minister.

The concession given by Gregory I to the priests of the diocese of Cagliari has been mentioned already.[75] Benedict XIV cites it as a precedent to show that for a grave reason the Pope can delegate a simple priest to confirm; and nearly all scholars are agreed now that it was the faculty to confirm that was conceded by Gregory.[76] So the point need not be labored.

The reason for the dispensation given by Gregory to the priests of Cagliari is important. As stated above, the Pope was informed that priests in the diocese of Cagliari were administering confirmation. He therefore sent them very definite instructions to

[74] *De Concordia Sacerdotii et Imperii* (4 vols., Neapoli, 1771), IV, 291.

[75] Cf. *supra,* Art. I.

[76] Tanquerey, *Synopsis Theologiae Dogmaticae* (3 vols., Vol. I-II, 24. 4d., Vol. III, 23. ed., Parisiis: Descle et Socii, 1934-1937), II, 403; Suarez, *Opera Omnia* (26 vols., Parisiis, 1856-1861), Vol. X, Quaestio LXXII, Art. XI; Bellarmine, *Opera Omnia* (12 vols., Parisiis, 1870-1874), Vol. IV, lib. II, cap. XII.

discontinue the practice. But apparently the prohibition of Gregory was not received with much favor. Scandal and disturbance were the result. Gregory therefore felt obliged to address another letter to these people, in which he stated:

> "It has come to our attention that certain people were scandalized, because we forbade priests to administer chrism on the forehead of those who had been baptized. And we indeed acted according to the ancient usage of our Church. But if some are really aggrieved on account of this, we permit that when bishops are absent priests may administer chrism even on the forehead."[77]

In his letter Gregory indicates the reason for the special concession he was making to the priests in Cagliari. It was because the people had been scandalized by the ruling of his earlier letter. However the custom of allowing simple priests to confirm had grown up in this diocese,[78] it must have been so well, or so long, established that any interference with it was considered a direct, unreasonable infringement on the rights of the priests and people. For that reason Gregory's first letter was ill received and there was scandal, probably on a large scale. To remove this occasion for scandal and consequent harm to souls, Gregory modified his earlier ruling and permitted priests to confirm, when bishops were not at hand.

It is hardly necessary to point out that Gregory had a grave reason for permitting the priests of Cagliari to confirm. Neither will the fact be overlooked that the priests were permitted to use their faculty only when bishops were not available. One has to conclude that there priests acted only in exceptional circumstances.

After the reign of Gregory there does not appear for a long time any concession allowing even an individual priest to adminis-

[77] *MPL,* LX, 144.

[78] It seems significant that the people of Cagliari were largely Greek, and that according to an established custom Greek priests were then confirming in the East.

ter confirmation in the Western Church, though particular councils found it necessary or advisable to insist that the faculty to confirm belonged in a very exclusive manner to bishops.[79] At the time of the revolt of Photius there was brought to the general attention of the West the common practice of priests confirming in the East. That this practice was really "extraordinary" will be noted in the next article. But in the West for many centuries the faculty of confirming was so rarely, if ever, given to priests that even distinguished theologians were holding that a priest as such simply could not in any circumstances be delegated to administer confirmation.[80]

In spite of the skepticism of Chardon,[81] it must be admitted that in the fourteenth, fifteenth and sixteenth centuries simple priests were given the faculty to confirm. For the facts and the circumstances no more convincing authority can be appealed to than Benedict XIV. In a *monitum* which Benedict (then Secretary of State) submitted to Clement XII in connection with a petition from South America, he cites Nicholas IV (1284-1292), John XII (1316-1334), Eugene IV (1413-1447), Leo X (1513-1521), Adrian XI (1522-1523) as having given the faculty to confirm to Franciscan priests sent to places in the north and east where there were no bishops.[82]

In the same place Benedict says that Gregory XIII (1572-1585) gave secular priests in Brazil the faculty to confirm, when no bishop could be obtained to confirm there.[83]

[79] Cf. Council of Seville (619), canon 7—Harduin, III, 560; Council of Paris (829), Lib. I, Cap. 27—Mansi, XIV, 556; Council of Worms (862), canon 8—Mansi, XV, 671.

[80] Albert the Great, *Commentaria in IV Sententiarum* (Parisiis, 1890-1899), Distinctio VII, Art. IV; Durandus, *In Petri Lombardi Sententias Theologicas Commentarium* (Venetiis, 1586), Lib. IV, Distinctio VII; cf. O'Dwyre, *Confirmation*, p. 163.

[81] *Histoire des Sacraments* (6 vols., Paris, 1745), I, 501.

[82] " . . . Fratres Minores, accedentibus ad partes orientis et septentrionis, ubi non reperiuntur episcopi."—*Thesaurus Resolutionum Sacrae Congregationis Concilii* (167 vols., Romae, 1718-1908), II, 187.

[83] Benedict's successor in the office of Secretary of State also cited the

In the instances just mentioned the faculty to confirm was given, as Benedict states, only to priests destined to work in places where no bishops were available to administer confirmation. The record of grants made even in such circumstances is very meager. The priest-minister therefore was regarded by the various popes quoted, in the same light in which he is regarded in modern canon law—as a minister for extraordinary circumstances.

In conformity with this doctrine is a statement contained in the Decree for the Armenians, and issued by Eugene IV. He writes: "It is read that by reason of a dispensation of the Apostolic See granted for a reasonable and grave cause simple priests have sometimes administered confirmation with chrism blessed by a bishop."[84]

A point that is of significance here is the fact that the Decree for the Armenians referred to the bishop as the *ordinary minister* of confirmation.[85] The implication seems to have been, even at that time, that a priest with the requisite delegation should be considered the extraordinary minister. At least there is evident a development, or clarification, of doctrine on the priest-minister.

In accordance with the practice of the Supreme Ecclesiastical Legislator concessions that were later made to simple priests to administer confirmation are notably rare; and in all cases the concessions were made only for grave reasons, which will presently be considered in detail. Here it seems opportune to mention briefly the dispensations given to abbots and prelates *nullius;* that is, as here understood, priests with a certain recognized dignity and an extensive jurisdiction,[86] but without episcopal orders. The faculty to confirm was given to the Abbot of Monte Cassino before the end of the sixteenth century.[87] In 1772 Clement XII gave the Abbot on Monte Virgine authority to confirm,

aforementioned pontiffs as having given priests the faculty to confirm. cf. *Thesaurus,* VI, 14.

[84] Denzinger, *Enchiridion,* n. 697.

[85] Cf. Denzinger, *Enchiridion,* n. 697.

[86] Cf. canons 323, 325.

[87] Cf. Benedict XIV, *De Synodo Dioecesana,* Lib. VII, cap. 8.

and a similar privilege was given to the Abbot of Cava.[88] The convenience and expedience of having the faculty of confirming attached to the offices of abbots and prelates *nullius* is very evident, considering the position of these ecclesiastics.

A more minute study of the causes for which the Holy See has been granting dispensations will now be attempted. By such a study one can better understand the precise circumstances in which the priest may be given the role of minister of confirmation.

The reasons for the probable dispensations given to priests in the fifth century have been noted already.[89] As regards the diocese of Cagliari, Gregory I stated very specifically the reason for the dispensation.[90] Minute details are not easily obtainable regarding the cases given on page 31; but in reference to these, it is perhaps sufficient to note that the faculty to confirm was there given to priests, because there was no bishop available.[91] The mind of the Holy See on the exact causes required for a dispensation is, however, clearly and precisely reflected in subsequent cases.

In a Chile case, which Cardinal Lambertini (then Secretary of State and afterwards Benedict XIV) prepared for the consideration of Clement XII, the renowned jurist writes as follows:

> "Although it is not simply and absolutely necessary, a grave and urgent cause is required in concessions of this kind, as may be understood from the Decree of Eugene IV.[92] There is also question of a dispensation; and every dispensation demands a cause. Moreover since Christ, our Lord, wished that the bishop should be the ordinary minister of this sacrament, it follows that there should not be another minister introduced without a grave cause . . . The cause required for this dispensation will not involve absolute necessity, since the the reception of this sacrament is not necessary for salvation;

[88] *Fontes,* n. 1972.
[89] Cf. Beginning of this Art.
[90] *Ep. XXVI—MPL,* LXXXIII, 820.
[91] Cf. *Thesaurus,* VI, 14.
[92] Denzinger, *Enchiridion,* n. 697.

> but in order that such a concession be considered necessary, it is sufficient that the inhabitants of some province (*provincia*), or even a large part of them, would have to go without confirmation for want of a minister."[93]

For more light on this point it is worth while citing part of an instruction sent to the Copts in the year 1745. It runs:

> "If indeed such is the condition of the Coptic people that confirmation cannot be administered to the faithful by bishops, to whom is committed the ordinary power of administering confirmation, we are aware that because of such need the faculty to confirm can sometimes be given to priests. It often happens that the faithful are without the solace of a pastor, and that because of the distance it is impossible or extremely difficult for bishops to get around to consult the needs of the people. In such circumstances priests are called upon to perform this part of the episcopal ministry (confirming) . . ., lest otherwise it should happen that the faithful, by having to wait, should neglect this source of sanctity, or die without this sacrament, filled with divine graces and instituted for our sanctification."[94]

Then the Instruction directed the Coptic missionaries to make a very careful study of the conditions in which the people lived, and to send a complete and conscientious report of their findings to the Holy See. This part of the Instruction deserves special attention, for it shows the pains the Holy See will take to investigate the alleged necessity, before it will delegate a priest to confirm. Note the wording:

> "The apostolic missionaries will therefore make a diligent and very careful inquiry to find out if the people have not a resident pastor; if the frequent visitation of the pastor is

[93] *Thesaurus,* II, 189.

[94] *Instructio super Dubiis ad Ritus Ecclesiae et Nationis Coptorum Pertinentibus,* 4 Maii, 1745—*Bullarium Pontificum Sacrae Cong. de Prop. Fide,* III, 191.

difficult or impossible; if he can minister to the people in case of necessity."

Note also the specific purpose for which they had to report to the Holy See:

"that the matter having been diligently, intimately and exhaustively considered, it could be determined whether and to whom, as extraordinary minister, the faculty to confirm should be granted."[95]

In this article have been cited and discussed a number of cases in which a priest was delegated to administer confirmation; parts of instructions and other important sources have been taken up and analyzed in an effort to determine as accurately as possible the attitude of the Holy See towards the extraordinary minister of confirmation. The study, confined almost exclusively to the West, shows that in the long course of the Church's history she has very rarely deputed simple priests to administer confirmation. It is also manifest that it was only for very grave reasons that she gave this authorization. Cardinal Lambertini in the Chile case intimated that *if the inhabitants of a province or a large part of them* would not be confirmed for want of a minister, there would be sufficient reason for delegating a simple priest. The instruction for the Copts would seem to demand a graver reason for dispensing in favor of them, else why would the Holy See insist on knowing if these people had spiritual opportunities, such as are afforded by a resident pastor, or frequent visitation of the pastor?

All this seems to prove that the priest is *by divine law* but the extraordinary minister of confirmation, as indeed seems to be implied in a canon which the Council of Trent enacted on the minister of confirmation.[96] The Church's lifelong practice also warrants the conclusion that a very grave cause is required in order that a simple priest may be delegated to administer confirmation.

[95] *Ibidem.*

[96] Canon 3, sess. VII, de *confirmatione.*

Article 3. Apparent Anomaly In Eastern Church

Amongst some of the Oriental Catholics there is a custom which is in apparent opposition to what has been said in article 1 and 2 regarding the ordinary and the extraordinary ministers of confirmation. According to this custom, prevalent amongst the majority of the peoples of the Eastern rites, a simple priest administers confirmation as a regular part of his sacerdotal duty.[97] After baptizing the children he immediately confirms them; though, if baptism is separated from confirmation, or if adults are to be confirmed, it is the bishop who confirms.[98] To explain this apparent inconsistency some little space must be given to the Eastern discipline, though of course this work is not directly concerned with the Orientals.

It cannot be alleged that the Eastern priests are ordinary ministers of confirmation, in the sense in which the word, ordinary, is here understood. The terms, *ordinary* and *habitual* are not synonymous, because as has been seen already the ordinary minister of confirmation is he who by virtue of his orders has the power to confirm; and, since simple priests have not that power by reason of their orders, it follows that they are not ordinary ministers of confirmation.[99]

Thus far there is no difficulty. But when one remembers the constant discipline of the Church reserving confirmation to bishops[100] and permitting priests to confirm only in exceptional cases and for very grave reasons, one naturally wonders why the Eastern practice is tolerated by Rome. Again we have a problem that demands an historical approach.

There are witnesses to show that for a number of centuries there was a general uniformity between the East and the West with regard to the minister of confirmation. In the third century St. Fermilian, who claims to speak for a large part of Asia Minor, assumed that it was only bishops who administered confirma-

[97] Cf. Cappello. *De Sacramentis, De Jure Ecclesiae Orientalis,* I, n. 853.

[98] Cappello, *ibidem.*

[99] Cf. Blat, *Commentarium,* Lib. III, Pars I, n. 79.

[100] Cf. Chap. I, Art. I.

tion.[101] In the next century St. John Chrysostom witnessed to a uniformity of discipline when he wrote: "Philip did not give the Holy Ghost, for he had not the faculty . . . This was a gift of the apostles alone . . . Therefore it was peculiar to the apostles. *Hence we see the highest ministers and not others doing it.*"[102] About the same time George Pachymeres appeared as another witness to the Eastern practice. Commenting on the Ecclesiastical History of Dionysius he writes: "Afterwards if anyone object: 'It (Christian initiation) is not fully effected by a priest, for a bishop was required to anoint the baptized person with chrism, because this was the ancient custom."[103] For some centuries, then, the general discipline of the East was in agreement with that of the West. But when, or how gradually the East departed from the earlier usage cannot be easily determined.[104]

In the fourth century a writer called Ambrosiaster stated that the Egyptian priests confirmed, if a bishop was not present.[105] About the same time the author of *Questions on the Old and the New Testament* wrote: "In Alexandria and throughout Egypt a priest confirmed, when a bishop was not present."[106] Probably this Alexandrian and Egyptian custom, noted as exceptional, was subsequently extended and became rather general in the East.[107]

At all events in the ninth century there is evidence of a seemingly general and long established custom permitting priests to confirm.[108] What reasons could have been alleged to justify such

[101] *Ep. LXXV*, c. 7—*Corpus Scriptorum Ecclesiasticorum Latinorum* (68 vols., editum consilio et impensis Academiae Litterarum Caesariae Vidobonae, 1866-), III, 814 ff. Henceforth this collection will have the abbreviation, "CSEL."

[102] *Hom. XVIII*—*MPG,* CLX, 144.

[103] *MPG,* III, 524.

[104] Cf. Souarn, "De Presbytero Orientali Confirmationis Ministro," *Jus Pontificium,* XI (1931), 137.

[105] *Commentaria in Epist. ad Ephesios. "Denique apud Aegyptum presbyteri consignant, si praesens not sit episcopus."*—*MPL,* XVII, 388.

[106] *MPL,* XXV, 232.

[107] Cf. Deslandes, "Le Pretre Oriental Ministre de la Confirmation," *Echos D'Orient,* XXIX (1930), 8.

[108] Cf. Photius, *Ep. III,* § 6, 7—*MPG,* CII, 725.

a custom are not apparent, but at least it escaped the condemnation of the Apostolic See, for Ratramnus, who was commissioned by Pope Nicholas to look into the Eastern situation and to reply to the charges of Photius,[109] was content to defend the Western reservation of confirmation to bishops by appealing to scripture and ancient tradition, without, however, asserting that the Eastern custom necessarily deserved condemnation.[110]

At the conclusion of the Council of Florence (1445) the question of priests' confirming in the East came up, and amongst the things the Greeks were asked to explain was this: "Why do the priests and not the bishops anoint with sacred chrism, since this is proper to the bishops?"[111] To this question, the Acts of the Council relate, the bishop of Mitilene gave a legitimate and satisfactory answer.[112]

We are not told what reasons the bishop of Mitilene alleged as a justification for priests' confirming in the East, nor are we told in so many words why Eugene IV was persuaded to allow the Orientals to continue their practice. The fact, however, that the question was raised shows that the West regarded the Eastern practice as anomalous, and the fact that after raising the question Rome abstained from condemning the Eastern custom shows that it judged there was sufficient reason to tolerate this exception to the general usage. Rome would have remembered the problem occasioned many centuries before, when she withdrew from the priests of Cagliari the faculty of confirming.[113] And so Eugene IV and his successors, who in their desire for reunion were so conciliatory with the Orientals,[114] permitted the Eastern priests to continue their practice. If Gregory I had conceded the priests of Cagliari the faculty to confirm, in order to remove an occasion of scandal, there is no reason why his successors could not have

[109] *Loc. cit.*

[110] *MPL,* CXX, 333.

[111] Harduin, X, 430.

[112] Harduin, *ibi.*

[113] Cf. Gregory I, *ep. XXVI—MPL,* LXXVII, 696.

[114] Cf. Sandalgi, "The Popes and the Christian East," *The Ecclesiastical Review,* LXXXVII (1932), 40-54.

given the same faculty in favor of a few million Orientals, who were so susceptible to scandal at any interference on the part of Rome. This explanation of the contrary Eastern usage shows that it can be reconciled with all that has been said in articles one and two regarding the ordinary and the extraordinary ministers of confirmation. It shows also that the Church is not inconsistent, when she tolerates the usage just considered.

CHAPTFR II

THREE QUESTIONS ON THE MINISTER OF CONFIRMATION

ARTICLE 1. SUBJECT OF POWER TO DELEGATE PRIESTS

The law on the extraordinary minister of Confirmation requires that he be delegated by the Apostolic See, and that in confirming he use chrism which has been blessed by a bishop.[1] Two questions therefore naturally arise: first, must the priest's delegation come *ex natura rei* from the Supreme Pontiff, and secondly, can a priest be delegated to bless the chrism? It seems that practical answers to these questions will result from a study of the practices that have always obtained regarding the blessing of chrism and the delegation of a priest for confirmation. As the heading indicates, this first article will be on the subject of the power to delegate priests for confirmation.

There is no question as to whether or not the bishops have at the present time the power to delegate a priest to confirm, for it is certain that the faculty to delegate is now so reserved to the Pope that a bishop is absolutely powerless to delegate.[2] The question is: does the delegation of a priest to confirm involve an exercise of power which belongs essentially to the Pope alone, and is necessarily not included in the power of a diocesan bishop?

Benedict XIV admits that, though the faculty to delegate is by law reserved to the Holy See, there is a basis for the view that in the absence of positive restriction, a bishop could give delegation to a priest to administer confirmation. The chief reason he gives for this opinion, after referring the reader to Lupus Christianus, are the canons cited in the preceding chapter to show that Spanish and Gallican councils gave to priests the authority to confirm.[3] The implication is that, if these priests received the

[1] Canons 782, § 2; 781, § 1.

[2] Cf. St. Thomas, *Summa*, q. LXXII, Art. XI, ad 1; Benedict XIV, *De Synodo Dioecesana*, Lib. VII, cap. 8, n. 7.

[3] *De Synodo Dioecesana*, Lib. VII, cap. 8, n. 3.

faculty to confirm, they received it not from the Pope but from the bishops acting in their ordinary official capacity, there being no hint that these councils might have received from the Pope the power to delegate priests to confirm. Apparently it was felt that the sévere ruling of Innocent I and Gelasius I would preclude the assumption that the bishops could have received any such commission from the Pope.[4]

In reference to the East, it is difficult to see how Innocent or Gelasius would have given even tacit consent to the Greek priests to administer confirmation as a part of their regular ministry.[5] Hence it is contended that the Eastern priests were authorized by their own bishops to confirm, and to this custom the Holy See afterwards acquiesced.[6]

An instruction sent by Benedict XIV to the Copts would seem to favor the opinion just expressed. Speaking of the Copts he says:

> "By a certain kindness and sufferance on the part of the Holy See it has happened that both sacraments (baptism and confirmation) have been administered amongst the Greeks in the Orient *by the same priest.* Nor are there wanting theologians who regard this toleration of the Holy See as having the character of a tacit dispensation."[7]

Here a distinction is made by Benedict between a certain sufferance and kindness on the one hand, and a tacit dispensation on the other. He says that *some* theologians interpreted the toleration and graciousness of the Holy See as a tacit dispensation. At most then there was only a tacit dispensation. But in saying that only some theologians held there was a tacit dispensation. Benedict implies that it was not necessary to admit even a tacit dispensation. Therefore it could be held that originally the Coptic priests confirmed with delegation received from their own bishops, and

[4] Cf. *MPL,* XX, 555; XIX, 50.
[5] Cf. *MPL,* XX, 555; LXXVII, 677.
[6] Cf. O'Dwyre, *Confirmation,* p. 169.
[7] *Bullarium Pontificum de Propaganda Fidei,* III, 190.

by the tacit permission of the Supreme Pontiff the Coptic practice was allowed to continue.

Yet, against the position that the bishop could *ex natura rei* delegate priests to confirm there are many difficulties. In the Decree for the Armenians occur these words: "It is read that sometimes *by delegation of the Apostolic See* . . . priests have administered the sacrament of confirmation."[8] Eugene IV was treating with the Orientals amongst whom confirmation had been administered for centuries by simple priests,[9] and yet he implies that he recognized priests had been able to confirm in the past, *only in so far as they had received from the Apostolic See the faculty to confirm.*[10]

In a questionnaire which Clement VI (1342-1352) sent to Consolator, patriarch of the Armenians, to test the orthodoxy of that ecclesiastic these questions occur:

> "Do you believe that it is only by the Roman Pontiff, who has the plentitude of power, that a dispensation to confirm can be given to simple priests? Do you believe that those confirmed by priests . . . who have not received for this a commission or some concession from the Roman Pontiff are to be again confirmed by a bishop?[11]

In the first question Clement apparently assumed that it is by reason of his plentitude of power that the Roman Pontiff delegates a simple priest to administer the sacrament of confirmation. That means it is by virtue of a power which is peculiar to him as Pope that he is able to commission a priest to confirm; and therefore no bishop by reason of his office or jurisdiction can give authorization to a priest to confirm.[12] The next question supposes that those who had been confirmed by a priest not delegated by

[8] Denzinger, *Enchiridion*, n. 697.

[9] Cf. Photius, *Ep. XIII—MPG*, CII, 725.

[10] Cf. Souarn, "De Presbytero Orientali Confirmationis Ministro," *Jus Pontificium*, XI (1931), 138 ff.

[11] Denzinger, *Enchiridion*, nn. 573-574.

[12] Cf. Deslandes, "Le Pretre Oriental la Ministre de la Confirmation," *Echos D'Orient*, XXIX (1930), 12 ff.

the Roman Pontiff should be again confirmed. To get the full implication of this question one has to understand that at this time priests were commonly administering confirmation in the East and in doing so they were apparently following a long established custom.[13] Ostensibly this custom might have owed its origin to a delegation of the Oriental priests by their own bishops, and the continuation of the practice might have been due to a negative or passive attitude on the part of the Holy See.[14] But, were that so, it could not have been said that the Eastern priests were confirming by virtue of a commission from the Pope. In Clement's second question, however, it is implied that a priest confirmed validly only when he had authorization from the Roman Pontiff; and so the bishop was not recognized as ever having had the power to delegate. Indeed both questions struck Benedict XIV so forcibly that he said those who would attribute the power of delegation to bishops (in the absence of reservation) had better take account of these questions of Clement.[15]

The theological reason that is given to show that this delegation of a priest is reserved essentially to the Pope is implicit in the following statement of St. Thomas:

> "In the Church the Pope has the plentitude of power by which he can commit to those in the lower orders certain functions that belong to those in the higher orders, as he gives certain priests the power to confer minor orders, though this belongs to the episcopal office. From this plentitude of power Pope Gregory gave simple priests the faculty to administer the sacrament of confirmation until scandal should be removed."[16]

From the reasons that have been presented for both sides of the controversy, it is evident that there cannot yet be absolute certainty for either position. But one thing is clear: the Church

[13] Cf. Photius, *Ep. XIII—MPG,* CII, 725.
[14] Cf. Tournely, *Theologia Moralis,* VIII, 170.
[15] *De Synodo Dioecesana,* Lib. VII, Cap. VIII, n. VII.
[16] *Summa Theologia,* Pars III, q. LXXII, art. XI, ad 1.

has very rarely, if ever, in her long history permitted a bishop *ex officio* to delegate priests to administer the sacrament of confirmation. For this reason, and particularly because it is only under compulsion, as it were,[17] that the Holy See has ever given a simple priest the faculty to confirm, it seems most probable that the Holy See will always reserve to itself the faculty to delegate priests to administer confirmation.

Article 2. The Priest and the Matter of Confirmation

One may ask is the blessing of chrism so reserved to the bishop that a priest cannot in any circumstances be delegated to bless it? Is it even in the power of the Roman Pontiff to delegate a priest?

The Decree for the Armenians which is very authoritative, though not definitive in all its parts, says: "The second sacrament is confirmation, the matter of which is chrism made up of oil . . . and balsam . . . *blessed by a bishop*."[18] It is indeed significant that Eugene IV used the phrase, *blessed by a bishop;* yet it is not agreed that Eugene IV has settled the question.[19] It remains therefore for the student to approach the matter from an historical angle, in order to see what further light can be obtained from a knowledge of the laws and practices that have obtained in the past.

On reading the legislation on the consecration of chrism, one is struck with the insistence and emphasis by which the consecration of chrism has been reserved to the bishop from the earliest time of which we have any record. In the decrees of the II Council of Carthage (390) we read:

> "It should be remembered that in the former councils it was laid down that the administration of chrism, or reconciliation of penitents, or consecration of virgins was not to be made by priests . . . By all the bishops it was established that

[17] Cf. "Instructio pro Simplici Sacerdote . . . . ", *AAS*, XXVII (1935), 13.

[18] Denzinger, *Enchiridion*, n. 697.

[19] Benedict XIV, *De Synodo Dioecesana*, Lib. VII, cap. 8, nn. 1-2.

> the blessing of chrism and the consecration of virgins should not be made by priests."[20]

This council held at a very early date refers back even to earlier councils by which it was decreed that the consecration of chrism was reserved to bishops. How far back the council points cannot be determined, but if one agrees with O'Dwyre, who defends the theory of a *specific* institution of the matter of confirmation by the Church, then one will probably accept the evidence he gives to show that chrism had not been used in confirmation long before this time.[21] Thus it may be supposed that from its adoption it was blessed by the bishop and none other.[22]

The III Council of Carthage (397) modified the ruling of the previous council on the reservation to priests of the consecration of women, but it definitely insisted that there was to be no change regarding the blessing of chrism. It decreed: "A priest is not to consecrate virgins without consulting the bishop, but *he is never to consecrate chrism.*"[23] In the previous canon it was seen that the consecration of virgins was, like the blessing of chrism, unconditionally reserved to the bishop and so one might have concluded that one function was reserved to the bishop with no greater rigidity than the other; but this latter council makes it understood that the blessing of chrism was much more strictly reserved to the bishop than the blessing of virgins.

Soon after the III Council of Carthage the Council of Toledo (400) issued the following important canon:

> "Although there is almost everywhere a custom that no one but a bishop blesses chrism, still because it is said that in some places, or provinces, priests bless the chrism, we command that from this day no one except a bishop shall bless the chrism, and for this diocese we further decree that deacons or subdeacons shall be deputed by each church to go to

[20] Canon 3—Harduin, I, 952.
[21] *Confirmation*, pp. 54 ff.
[22] Cf. Letter of Montanus—Harduin, I, 44.
[23] Canon 36—Harduin, I, 964.

the bishop before Easter and obtain some of the chrism blessed by him for Easter."[24]

The council admits that there were some rare exceptions to the practice that bishops alone blessed the chrism. But the council made it known that it was not going to tolerate any exception in future; and effectively to guard against any recurrence of the abuse, the priests were told definitely how they were to procure chrism for use in their churches.

Important as the testimony of these councils is, there is even more important testimony available in the decrees of the popes of the period. Innocent I (400-417) permitted priests to anoint baptized people with chrism, but he made the express stipulation that the chrism should be consecrated by a bishop.[25] Amongst the evidently gross abuses for which Gelasius I severely reproved the priests of Lucania was the blessing of chrism.[26] Thus we see that while Innocent permits priests to administer chrism as a sacrament, he is very careful to have the priests understand that the chrism must have been blessed by a bishop. And from the tone of the letter of Gelasius one must conclude that he regarded the blessing of chrism as an unprecedented arrogation of authority on the part of the priests of Lucania.

About the beginning of the sixth century, Montanus, Archbishop of Toledo, wrote an extraordinary letter to Theoribus. It reads in part:

"We have taken care to communicate to you certain abuses in order that by your reproof such arrogance may not occur in the future. Certain priests, it is related to us, have in the most rash manner presumed not to consecrate, but rather to profane, sacred things. They have, in a fashion and with a foolhardiness I cannot describe, brazenly grasped for themselves a prerogative denied the highest of their class, since the beginning of the Catholic religion, and belonging only to

[24] Canon 20—Harduin, I, 992.
[25] *MPL,* XX, 555.
[26] *MPL,* XLIX, 50.

bishops: that is, the right of blessing chrism. How sacrilegious this is does not escape your upright conscience I am sure; and therefore I hope that to eradicate this evil you will use the authority of a most zealous priest, and coerce those who profane such a sacred thing."[27]

When a letter of such severity comes from the pen of an archbishop in any century, one can form some idea of the seriousness of the abuse which it was intended to have corrected. Nothing could have shown more strikingly than this letter that the blessing of chrism was most strictly reserved to bishops.

The authorities continued to forbid priests to consecrate chrism, and they laid down severe penalties for a violation of the law. A council in Braga (561) commanded them not to do it under penalty of deposition: "If any priest after this prohibition shall dare to bless chrism . . . he shall be deposed from his office, because from ancient times the canons have forbidden this."[28]

The Council of Seville also (619) prohibited priests to bless the chrism, because, as it said, they lacked the dignity of bishops.[29]

The blessing of chrism was all along so consistently reserved to the bishops that before the middle of the fifteenth century there does not occur even an alleged instance of priests legitimately receiving the faculty to bless chrism. A record in the Annals of the Friars Minor, however, states that in 1444 Fabian de Bacchia and many of his fellow religious were given the faculty to bless chrism.[30] This was supposed to have been given by Eugene IV, but there is some question as to its genuinity,[31] and the fact that there is reference to it again in a recent compilation of Franciscan bulls is not conclusive proof.[32] It does not seem prob-

[27] Harduin, I, 44.

[28] Canon 7—Harduin, III, 352.

[29] Harduin, III, 559.

[30] Tournely gives the reference as n. 45 for the year 1444 in the Annals of the Friars Minor as compiled by Waddingus.

[31] Cf. Benedict XIV, *De Synodo Dioecesana,* Lib. VII, cap. 8, n. 2.

[32] "Sacrae Religionis Inquisitori Fratri, Fabiano de Bacchia, Ordinis Minorum, in partibus septentrionalibus Molaviae, Walachiae, Bulgariae

able that a faculty that had been so long and so strictly reserved to bishops would be thus given to several priests[33] on one occasion. If the Pope saw fit to grant the faculty to a priest at all, it seems that it would have been sufficient to give it to one or two missionaries. That would have been more in accord with the conservative attitude of the Holy See. Besides, this alleged concession was given by Eugene IV, the very Pontiff who stated in his Decree for the Armenians that the matter of confirmation is *chrism blessed by a bishop.*[34]

When the Holy See gives a priest the faculty to confirm in some extraordinary circumstances, it always stipulates that the chrism used must have been blessed by a bishop.[35] And though the Church has given the abbot and prelate *nullius* without episcopal orders the right to bless chalices and patens, to administer confirmation and minor orders, to consecrate churches and altars, she does not give them authority to bless chrism.[36]

From this brief review of the laws and practices regarding the consecration of chrism, it is evident that the Church has always insisted most strongly that the prerogative of blessing chrism was reserved to bishops in a peculiar, very probably an exclusive, manner. It seems really doubtful if the faculty to bless chrism was ever given to a simple priest. Whether or not the Church has the power to commission a priest to consecrate chrism cannot be proved by any certain precedent.

Article 3. Heretical and Schismatical Ministers

A matter of practical and not purely historical interest is the Church's lifelong attitude to confirmation administered by schismatical and heretical ministers. Did the Church in the early cen-

. . . concedimus facultatem ut omnes et singuli fratres possunt Eucharistiae, Baptismatis, chrismatis, seu confirmationis . . . oleum sanctum et chrisma benedicere et conficere."—Bullarium Franciscanum, I, n. 5631.

[33] Cf. preceding footnote.

[34] Denzinger, *Enchiridion*, n. 697.

[35] Cf. *AAS,* XXVII (1935), 16; *Bullarium Pontificum de Sac. Cong. de Prop. Fide,* III, 190.

[36] Cf. Canon 323, § 2.

turies administer confirmation indiscriminately to all converts from heresy? What position do we see the Church holding in more recent centuries with regard to confirmation received from heretical ministers? Opposite views have been held on the question of the validity of confirmation received from heretical ministers, the negative view being based chiefly on the Church's alleged confirmation of *all* converts from heresy during the early centuries. It must be admitted that the facts of history bearing on this matter present considerable difficulty. A presentation of these facts will reveal what the difficulties are, and an examination of them will show what, if any, definite inference can be drawn from them.

In the celebrated controversy between St. Cyprian of Carthage and Pope St. Stephen, it appears that the Pope ordered confirmation to be administered to all convert heretics. Cyprian had denied the validity of heretical baptism, and made it a practice to baptize all converts from heresy. The Pope condemning Cyprian's practice sent the following command:

> "If anyone therefore come to you from any heresy whatsoever, let nothing be innovated which has not been handed down, that hands should be imposed on him for penance, since the heretics themselves do not baptize such as come to them from one another, but admit them to communion."[37]

The passage in itself does not indeed seem to be an unmistakable reference to confirmation, because, at least in the form that has come down to us, it reads: hands should be imposed for *penance.* However, it is certain that it was understood to refer to confirmation by Cyprian of Carthage and by other recognized authorities who presumably were not deceived. Cyprian writes:

> "If they attribute the effect of baptism to the majesty of the name, so that those who are baptized anywhere and anyhow in the name of Jesus Christ, are judged to be renewed and sanctified, why do not the baptized persons in the name of the same Christ, *receive the imposition of hands there* (in the

[37] *CSEL,* III, 799.

> heretical sect) *for the reception of the Holy Ghost?* Why does not the same majesty of the same name avail *in the imposition of hands* which, they contend, availed in the sanctification of baptism."[38]

Cypian thinks that the Pope and those who agreed with him in admitting the validity of heretical baptism, but in requiring an imposition of hands, were utterly inconsistent; and the value of Cyprian's argument depends entirely on this alleged inconsistency. "If," Cyprian argues, "it be granted that heretics baptize validly, then consistency demands that it be also admitted that they impose hands, or confirm, validly." Cyprian therefore evidently understands the Pope to refer to confirmation; otherwise he could have no charge of inconsistency, and his argument would be absurd. Besides, when Cyprian speaks of a mere reconciliation ceremony, there is no mistaking his meaning. He writes, for example:

> "Which ancient custom we observe in the present day, that it is sufficient to impose hands for penance upon those who are known to have been baptized in the Church, if subsequently acknowledging their error they return to the truth and their parent."[39]

Clearly, to this ceremony Cyprian does not attribute the power to give the Holy Ghost, as he does to the ceremony ordered by Stephen. There can be no doubt therefore about Cyprian's understanding of the Pope's words.

Firmilian, Bishop of Caesarea in Cappadocia and a contemporary of Cyprian, is of the same impression regarding the imposition of hands prescribed by Stephen. Nor is Firmilian less clear than the metropolitan of Carthage. He writes:

> "All power and grace are established in the Church where the elders preside, who possess not only the power of baptizing but also that of the imposition of hands, and of or-

[38] *CSEL,* III, 802-803.
[39] *CSEL,* III, 799.

> daining. For as a heretic may not lawfully ordain nor lay on hands, so neither can he baptize . . . all which we some time back confirmed in Iconium, a place in Phrygia, when we were assembled together with those who had gathered from Galatia, and Cilicia and other neighboring countries, as to be held and firmly vindicated against heretics, when there was some doubt in certain minds concerning the matter. And as Stephen and those who agree with him contend the putting away of sin and second birth may result from the baptism of heretics, among whom they themselves confess the Holy Ghost is not, let them consider and understand that the *spiritual* birth cannot be without the spirit . . ."[40]

After this Firmilian goes on to say sarcastically that the bishops who would impose hands on heretics without first baptizing them must consider themselves more powerful than St. Paul, who was obliged to baptize the Ephesians before he could confirm them. In the passage cited verbatim Firmilian puts the three actions, ordaining, laying on of hands, baptizing in the same category. This is a certain indication that he has confirmation in mind. He regards the imposition of hands ordered by Stephen to be made on the converts from heresy as the same imposition of hands that St. Paul made on the Ephesians. This is another convincing proof that Firmilian, like his brother bishop in Carthage, believed Stephen to have ordered confirmation for converts from heresy.

Even a writer who was on the side of Stephen in the baptismal dispute understood the imposition of hands on heretics in precisely the same sense as Cyprian and Firmilian understood it. The author of *De Rebaptismate* has this to say:

> "I observe that it has been asked among the brethren what rules should specially be adopted in regard to those who, though baptized in heresy, should repent with their whole hearts and implore from the Church the help of salvation; whether according to the most ancient and ecclesiastical tradition it would suffice, after that baptism which they had re-

[40] *Ep. LXXV*, c. 7—*CSEL*, III, 814-815.

ceived outside, indeed, but still in the name of Jesus Christ, our Lord, that hands alone should be imposed on them by the bishop for the reception of the Holy Ghost, and the imposition of hands would thus afford them the renewal and perfected seal of faith, or whether indeed a repetition of baptism would be necessary for them."[41]

What reference to confirmation could be more explicit than this? An imposition of hands for the reception of the Holy Ghost was long the common way of designating the act of confirming.[42] In answering the question the author uses the same kind of wording.

> "If it (baptism) should have been administered by strangers, let this matter be amended as it can and as it allows. Because outside the Church there is no Holy Ghost, even faith cannot exist either among heretics or among those who are established in schism. And for that reason those who do penance and are amended by the doctrine of the truth and by their faith which has subsequently been corrected and improved by the purification of heart, should be aided only by spiritual baptism: that is, by the imposition of the bishops hands and by the administration of the Holy Ghost."[43]

The three witnesses cited as interpretative of Stephen's decree cannot be easily gainsaid, particularly when it is realized that they did not represent the opinion of only one place, and that they were neither in common agreement with, nor in common opposition to, Stephen in the prevailing struggle. It is not easy to imagine that they could have been deceived regarding the nature of the reconciliation ceremony ordered by Stephen. Subsequent legislation and practice, moreover, seems to corroborate the understanding these men had of the force of the imposition of hands under consideration.

The Council of Arles (314) enacted this law on the reconciliation of heretics:

[41] *MPL,* III, 1185-1186.
[42] Cf. Saintebeuve, *De Confirmatione,* pp. 1-4.
[43] *MPL,* III, 1195.

> "In regard to the Africans who use their own law of rebaptism, it hath seemed good that, if anyone comes to the Church from this heresy, let them examine him on the symbol; and if they learn that he has been baptized in the Father, Son and Holy Ghost, let hands alone be imposed on him for the reception of the Holy Ghost. But if when examined he does not mention the Trinity, let him be baptized."[44]

This canon uses the same terminology as the writer quoted above, and therefore the canon is to be interpreted in the same manner as those writers have been interpreted. It may be noted in passing, however, that the Council specifies exactly the kind of heretics that are to be initiated by an imposition of hands for the reception of the Holy Ghost. Perhaps the council visualizes heretics who would have to be received in a different way, for the reason that the confirmation they received in heresy was considered valid. It may be helpful to keep this in mind in an investigation to be made later to see if *all* heretics were confirmed on coming into the Catholic Church.

The I General Council of Constantinople (381) also seems to prescribe confirmation for heretics entering the Church. The essential part of canon 7 reads:

> "We receive the Arians when they make a formal petition and renounce all heresy, which is not in agreement with the Holy Catholic and Apostolic Church of God. And having signed or anointed them first with the holy chrism, we sign on the forehead, eyes, nose and ears saying: 'The sign of the gift of the Holy Spirit'."[45]

The anointing mentioned and the concomitant words certainly look like the administration of the sacrament of confirmation. It is exactly similar to the confirmation ceremony used today in the Greek Church.[46] For this canon, however, we are fortunate to have the interpretation of one of the most eminent canonists,

[44] Mansi, II, 472.
[45] Mansi, III, 563.
[46] Cf. Cappello, *De Sacramentis,* I, n. 842.

Benedict XIV. He says that this canon refers to heretics who did not confer the sacrament of confirmation at all, or conferred it invalidly.[47]

As the centuries passed, the same form of initiation for heretics was insisted on: a form which seems to indicate the conferring of the Holy Ghost. About the middle of the fifth century Pope Leo I wrote to the bishop of Ravena:

> "But if it be proved that anyone has been baptized by heretics, in such a case let there be no approach to a repetition of the sacrament of regeneration, but let that only be conferred which was absent there, namely, *that through the imposition of the bishop's hand he may obtain the power of the Holy Ghost.*"[48]

Here again there could be no plainer reference to the sacrament of confirmation to be conferred on heretics.

In this place a word of explanation may be necessary regarding two conciliatory ceremonies that seem very different from each other but are essentially the same. At one time we see heretics are to be reconciled to the Church by a sealing to which the power of giving the Holy Ghost is attributed, at another time we note that the reconciliation is to be affected by an imposition of hands, which is likewise considered to impart the Holy Ghost. One explanation is that two phrases might be used indiscriminately to designate the same thing, that is, confirmation.[49] The more precise explanation seems to be that, where at the time in question unction was used in confirmation, the authorities speak of an anointing as the reconciliation ceremony. Holding the theory of only a generic institution of the matter of the sacrament of confirmation by Christ, O'Dwyre produces weighty arguments to show that, when the use of chrism in the administration of confirmation had become general in the East, the West was still con-

[47] *Bullarium Sacrae Congregationis de Prop. Fide,* III, 425.
[48] *MPL,* LIV, 1094.
[49] Cf. Saintebeuve, *De Sacramento Confirmationis,* pp. 1-4.

firming with an imposition of hands without the use of chrism.[50] This shows that it makes no material difference whether a canon refers to a reconciliation ceremony as an imposition of hands or as an anointing with chrism. If one ceremony is confirmation, it does not follow that the other is not.

A cursory survey of all the early legislation on the reconciliation of heretics might give the impression that the Church for a number of centuries confirmed all converts from heresy, even though these heretics had in most instances already submitted to a confirmation rite in an heretical church. That is apparently why the belief had obtained among a number of scholars that confirmation administered by heretical ministers was always invalid.[51]

But was there a wholesale confirmation of converts from heresy in the early Church, even when, as we may presume, converts came from a sect in which the proper matter and form of confirmation were used? What reasonable explanation do we find upon careful and exhaustive study of the facts? It does not seem that the solution of the difficulty can be based on the fact that the sacramental nature of confirmation was not sufficiently unfolded. The Church or a number of important councils must have had the ability to determine what was essential for confirmation, before theologians arose to make a thorough analysis of this sacrament. The solution Chardon gives also seems inadmissible.[52] He submits the view that the Church frequently did reconcile or initiate heretics by a rite that was very much like the rite of confirmation, but it was not really confirmation, because the minister

[50] *Confirmation,* Chap. V.

[51] O'Dwyre lists the following writers as denying the validity of confirmation administered by heretical ministers: Maldonatus, *De sacramentis,* tom. I, *De Confirmatione,* q. 1, 2; Morinus, *De Poenitentia,* Lib. I, Cap. XII, XIII, XIV; Hefele, *History of the Councils,* Vol. I, p. 112; Schanz. *Die Lehre von den heiligen Sacramenten der katholischen Kirche,* p. 287, n. 6; Duchesne, *Origines du Culte Cretien,* p. 327; Saltet, *Lex Reordinations,* p. 18-20, 402-406; Pourat, *Theology of the Sacraments* (English Translation), p. 208-213; *Dictionnaire de Theologie Catholique,* tom. III, p. 409.

[52] *Histoire de la Confirmation,* Chap. V, in fine.

had not the intention of administering the sacrament. The intention of the minister does indeed determine the sacramental act[53] but the wording of all the prescriptions above cited on the reconciliation of heretics seems to denote confirmation, or the giving of the Holy Ghost, so explicitly that Chardon's theory cannot be admitted without the danger of doing violence to the texts in question. It is necessary to seek another solution which will be more reasonable in itself, and which will safeguard the Supreme Ecclesiastical Authority as a consistent legislator and as an unerring judge in the matter of the validity of a sacrament. It appears that a better examination of the evidence available will show that confirmation was not invariably administered to converts from heresy and that in the period under consideration the Church did distinguish heresy from heresy, and did recognize in some cases the validity of confirmation administered by heretics, just as she does today.

St. Optatus (4th century) in his book, *Contra Parmenianum*, seems to have no doubt about the validity of confirmation administered by heretical ministers under due conditions. The Donatists in their antagonism had called the Catholics dying flies that contaminate the sacred oil. To this Optatus replied:

> "Do we set at naught your unction, by again anointing those whom you have anointed, as if they had not been anointed at all? By no means. But if anyone pass over from you to us, he is accepted as he came from you . . . If we should hold inane the oil administered by you, rightly indeed could you call us dying flies; but while we hold what was anointed by you as we received it from you, we cannot be called dying flies."[54]

These statements have a figurative dress, it is true, but it seems that the only natural and obvious interpretation is that they refer to confirmation. From this it follows that the authoritative writer just cited admitted the validity of heretical confirmation administered in certain circumstances.

[53] Cf. Tanquerey, *Synopsis Theologiae Dogmaticae,* III, n. 416 ff.
[54] Lib. VII, Cap. IV, *Contra Parmenianum—MPL,* XI, 1088-1099.

A short time after Optatus St. Augustine himself appears with an assertion on the validity of heretical confirmation. In his book, *De Baptismo,* he refutes the arguments of Cyprian for the invalidity of heretical baptism. Then to the Donatists, who objected: "How can a homicide cleanse and sanctify water? How can darkness (heretical ministers) bless oil?" St. Augustine replies: "If God be present in the sacrament and in His words, then the sacraments of God are everywhere valid, by whomsoever they may be administered."[55] These words from the pen of St. Augustine are particularly convincing, not merely because of his recognized authority in all matters ecclesiastical, but especially because in his controversies with the Donatists he was obliged to make a close study of the nature of the sacraments. Hence he would have been well qualified to give a sound opinion on the heretical minister's capacity in the administration of valid confirmation.

Gregory I, speaking of a long period that preceded his time, mentions the different ways by which the Church was wont to take back heretics. His words seem a clear indication that the Church sometimes received heretics by a rite that was sacramental, and sometimes by a rite that was decidedly not sacramental. He writes:

> "And indeed from the ancient institution of the Fathers we have learned that those who were baptized in the name of the Trinity among heretics, when they return to the Holy Church are received to the bosom of the Church either by an imposition of hands or by a mere profession of faith."[56]

All the heretics referred to in this passage were baptized in heresy, and presumably brought up in heresy. There can be no question therefore of the use of a profession of faith to reconcile *former Catholics* who had lapsed into heresy. Why then the imposition of hands or unction in one instnace, and a mere profession of faith in the other? It seems more than probable that it

[55] *MPL,* XLIII, 149.
[56] *MPL,* LXXVII, 1204.

was because the Church would not confirm some heretics, because she considered them to have been validly confirmed already; and she confirmed others, because in their case she noted a lack of something essential to the sacrament.

To sum up now the discussion of the early period about which there has been so much dispute, it does not appear from the facts or legislation taken on the whole that the Legislator, who today recognizes the validity of heretical confirmation, can be charged with any inconsistency or with any error in the evaluation of heretical confirmation. Though some writers have based their belief that heretical confirmation is invalid chiefly on the alleged early practice of the Church's confirming all converts from heresy, the evidence and authority of Augustine, Optatus and Gregory is, it seems, convincing proof that the Church did not in theory or practice deny the validity of heretical confirmation, *suppositis supponendis.* The Church distinguished. She found heretical confirmation to be invalid in some instances for want of some essential element, and in such a case she confirmed. In other instances she found that heretical confirmation had the required elements, and therefore she abstained from a repetition of the ceremony.

In the consideration of the Church's attitude towards confirmation administered by heretical ministers in more recent times, the practical question concerns confirmation administered by schismatical (or heretical) Greek priests. The decisions and the norms that the Holy See has given with regard to these ministers will enable one to solve most questions that may now arise in reference to the validity of confirmation outside the Church.

After Photius broke with the Church, he sent a number of his priests to work in Bulgaria, and these administered confirmation to many of the Bulgarians. But Pope Nicholas hearing of this sent bishops to confirm the Bulgarians who had been confirmed by the schismatical Greek priests. This might have been taken as an indication that the Pope judged the schismatical priests to be without the power to confirm. There are, however, other explanations which are given by Benedict XIV.[57] He says that Nicholas

[57] *De Synodo Dioecesana,* Lib. VII, cap. 9.

wished to have the Bulgarians confirmed again, (1) because they had received confirmation from priests who, imbued with the error of Photius, confirmed as by ordinary right, that is thinking that the power to confirm was in the same way common to priests and bishops; (2) because these priests had been delegated by Photius, who was a traitor and intruder—in other words a pseudo-patriarch to whom the rights of a legitimate patriarch did not belong; (3) because Bulgaria belonged to the Western patriarchate, and therefore the delegation which had been expressly or tacitly conceded by the Holy See to the Greek priests to administer confirmation in the eastern patriarchate by no means authorized them to do the same thing in Bulgaria.

Passing over many centuries in which there is nothing of special importance bearing on the present section, one may profitably take up a very important response given by the Holy Office in 1853. The following two questions were submitted to it:

> "(1) If a schismatic returns to the unity of the Church and, there being no people with whom he can practice the Greek rite, he embraces the Latin rite (intending to remain a layman and not to become a priest), may the bishop of the Latin rite confirm him conditionally? (2) If children of Catholic parents are baptized by schismatics, may the Latin bishop confirm them again conditionally?" The reply reads: "It is not expedient that those confirmed by schismatic priests should be again confirmed."

Then followed a very important and instructive Ad Mentem:

> "The understanding is that in particular cases the bishop should find out the exact place in which the converts had been confirmed. If it was in Bulgaria or the Island of Cyprus, in Italy or the adjacent islands, or amongst the Lebanon Maronites, or in some place where the faculty to confirm was not expressly revoked the people are not to be disturbed. In doubt, however, about the place or the mode or some other important circumstances, recourse should be made to the Holy See."[58]

[58] *Collectanea S.C.P.F.*, I, 1095.

This response shows that in certain territories where there was no explicit revocation of the faculty to confirm, heretical priests still enjoy it. Thus, too, is furnished a norm by which can be settled nearly all doubts that may arise regarding the validity of confirmation given by Greeks outside the Church. It is true indeed that there are other later responses in the *Collectanea* of the Congregation for the Propagation of the Faith on the question of the validity of confirmation administered by schismatics. But the reason for these subsequent questions was, it seems, uncertainty as to whether or not the faculty to confirm had ever been conceded to priests in certain places, or, if conceded, whether or not it had been revoked. With regard to Jerusalem to which two of the responses had reference, Benedict XIV had said long before that it was really doubtful if the power to confirm had ever been given to the priests of the Church of Jerusalem.[59] Further discussion of these responses is therefore unnecessary.[60]

From the foregoing it can be seen that confirmation administered by heretical ministers was in some instances, apparently many instances, considered invalid. The reasons for its being judged invalid are not indicated, but it is certain that it was not because of any lack of power on the part of the heretical minister as such. It is sufficiently clear from the facts considered that heretical confirmation was in some instances accepted by the Church as valid. And as to the Eastern schismatical ministers, there is a safe general guide in the response of 1853.

[59] *De Synodo Dioecesana,* Lib. III, cap. 9, n. 4.

[60] Several of these responses are discussed in another connection, Chap. IV, Art. 9.

Part Two
CANONICAL COMMENTARY

Chapter III

POWERS, RIGHTS AND OBLIGATIONS OF THE ORDINARY MINISTER

Article 1. Summary of Doctrinal Development

In earlier Christian times, before the general evolution of sacramental theology, no explicit distinction was made between an ordinary and an extraordinary minister of confirmation; or between a minister who by virtue of his ordination alone was competent, and a minister who in addition to his sacramental order needed also a special commission. Yet, as the study pursued in Chapter I reveals, the Church has always insisted that in ordinary circumstances the administration of confirmation is the peculiar prerogative of the bishop. The forthright action of Pope Nicholas I (858-867) with regard to Bulgaria demonstrated not only the strictness with which the administration of confirmation was reserved to the bishop, but also the exclusive competence of the bishop to confirm without special authorization.[1] The decree *Exultate Deo*[2] of Pope Eugene IV (1431-1447) was the first ecclesiastical document to state in express terms that the bishop is the *ordinary* minister of confirmation,[3] though subsequent to its issuance there was not unanimity regarding the sense in which the word "ordinary" was to be taken.[4] Did it admit or did it rule out the possibility of an extraordinary minister? That question was raised long after the Council of Florence:[5] and it was debated amongst theologians even after the Council of Trent.[6] The weight of authority was indeed in favor of an interpretation of Eugene IV which agrees fully with the doctrine clearly and explicitly set

[1] Cf. Deslandes, *"Le Pretre Oriental Ministre de la confirmation," Echos d'Orient*, XXIX (1930), 14; Tournely, *op. cit.*, VIII, 303.

[2] Nov. 22, 1439; cf. Denzinger, *Enchiridion*, n. 695.

[3] Cf. Denzinger, *Enchiridion*, n. 697.

[4] Cf. O'Dwyre, *Confirmation*, p. 164.

[5] Cf. Benedict XIV, *De Synodo Dioecesana*, Lib. VII, cap. VII, n. IV.

[6] Cf. Saintebeuve, *Tractatus de Sacramento Confirmationis*, p. 445.

forth in the present Code.[7] Yet at the Council of Trent itself there was diversity of opinion amongst the Fathers and consulting theologians, and it was only after some hesitation and difficulty that the correct Catholic doctrine was formulated and defined.[8] Even then a certain caution was manifested, for there was no explicit statement regarding an extraordinary minister. So evident was this non-committal attitude regarding a priest-minister that Saintbeuve could hold in his book on confirmation published in 1778 that the bishop was the strictly exclusive minister of confirmation.[9]

Eventually, and perhaps chiefly on account of the influence of Benedict XIV,[10] complete Catholic agreement was established with regard to the meaning intended in the first canon of the Council of Trent on Confirmation. At present there is no controversy. A representative modern canonist says: "By the ordinary minister of confirmation is meant one who in virtue of an order received has by divine law the power to act ordinarily as the minister of confirmation."[11] The ordinary minister, then, is not the exclusive minister; but he is distinguished from the extraordinary minister because by the divine law he derives his competence from an order (episcopate) received, and because in the exercise of his faculty he is not restricted to unusual or extraordinary conditions.

Article 2. Interpretation of Canon 782, §1

Canon 781 § 1: *Ordinarius confirmationis minister est solus Episcopus.*

The first paragraph of canon 782 is a literal restatement of the doctrine formulated and enjoined under penalty of anathema by the Council of Trent.[12] In both cases it is stated that the bishop

[7] Canon 782.

[8] Cf. Pallavicino, *Vera Concilii Tridentini Historia* (3 vols., Antverpiae, 1670), Lib. IX, cap. 7, n. 11 ss.

[9] Cf. *Tractatus de Sacramento Confirmationis,* p. 445.

[10] Cf. *De Synodo Dioecesana,* Lib. VII, cap. VII, nn. IV-VII.

[11] Blat, *Commentarium,* III, Pars I, n. 76.

[12] Sess. VII, *de confirmatione,* can. 3—Denzinger, *Enchiridion,* n. 873.

alone, and therefore no one else, is the ordinary minister of confirmation. The bishop, in virtue of his episcopal consecration without any regard to jurisdiction or orthodoxy or favor of the Apostolic See or the will of the Apostolic See, can always administer the sacrament of confirmation validly.[13] The law makes no distinction. Neither does our previous historical study require a distinction to be made. In Chapter 1, Article 3, it has been demonstrated that heretical and schismatical bishops are capable of giving confirmation validly. Though all jurisdiction be withdrawn from these bishops by the Supreme Ecclesiastical Authority, they are still able to confirm validly. By no power which the Pope possesses can bishops be deprived of their faculty to confirm. On this point the authors are agreed.[14]

That the Church could deprive a bishop of the power to bless chrism, which is the essential matter of confirmation, is a theory advanced by Lehmkuhl.[15] If that view could be sustained, the Church could prevent the matter of confirmation from being available to heretical and schismatical bishops, and thus they would be indirectly divested of their faculty to confirm.

Lehmkuhl's theory is based on another theory, namely, that the Church has considerable power over the matter of the sacraments, so that She could stipulate, for example, not merely that chrism consecrated by a bishop would be the essential matter of confirmation, but she could condition the validity of the matter on a bishop's standing with Rome.[16] It remains however for some theologian to demonstrate that the Church has such very extensive power over the matter of confirmation. As yet no convincing proof has been offered.[17] On the contrary, a statement of Pope

[13] Cf. Hinschius, *System des katholischen Kirchenrechts* (4 vols., Berlin, 1869-1888), IV, 55.

[14] Cf. Suarez, *Opera Omnia*, Vol. XX, Quaest. LXXII, Art. XI, Sec. I, n. 1; Lehmkuhl, *Theologia Moralis*, II, n. 35; Wernz-Vidal, *Ius Canonicum*, Tom. IV, Vol. I, n. 55.

[15] Cf. O'Dwyre, *Confirmation*, p. 127.

[16] Cf. McDonald, "The Sacrament of Extreme Unction," *ITQ*, II (1907), 339.

[17] Cf. Tanquerey, *Synopsis Theologiae Dogmaticae*, III, n. 333 ff.

Pius X denies that the Church has extensive power over the matter of the sacraments.[18]

An attempt has been made, it is true, to show that in early Christian times an imposition of the bishop's hands without the use of chrism was considered sufficient for a valid confirmation, and that only at a later date did the Church require chrism as the essential matter of confirmation.[19] Such an opinion which in opposition to the common teaching gives the Church such very extensive power over the matter of the sacrament may well be taken to support the view that the Church could determine the matter of confirmation to be chrism blessed by a bishop *having jurisdiction.* Heretical and schismatical bishops would then for want of jurisdiction be incapable of blessing chrism, and to that extent they would be restrained from confirming validly. Until however the alleged extensive power of the Church over the matter of some of the sacraments by Christ has been commonly accepted, Lehmkuhl's theory cannot be taken as valid proof that the Church can even indirectly deprive heretical and schismatical bishops of their power to confirm.

The fact that a validly consecrated bishop has the power to confirm validly does not mean that confirmation administered by heretical and schismatical bishops is necessarily valid.[20] There are, apart from the minister's powers of orders, other elements on which the validity of the sacrament is equally dependent. The intention of the minister which will frequently be influenced by his doctrine with regard to the sacrament of confirmation is a very important element.[21] If he believes with the Lutherans that confirmation is a purely ceremonial imposition of hands connected with a profession of faith,[22] he may not have the intention re-

[18] Ep. *"Ex quo,"* 26 dec. 1910: " . . . Cum tamen compertum sit Ecclesiae minime competere ius circa ipsam sacramentorum substantiam quidpiam innovandi . . . "—*AAS,* III (1911), 119.

[19] O'Dwyre, *Confirmation,* p. 184.

[20] Cf. Chap. II, Art. 3.

[21] Cf. Tanquerey, *Synopsis Theologiae Dogmaticae Fundamentalis,* III, nn. 418-421.

[22] Cf. Tanquerey, *op. cit.,* III, n. 553.

quired for the valid administration of the sacrament. Besides, unless he uses the essential form, and the essential remote and proximate matter, the sacrament will not be valid. To a defect or a suspected defect of this kind must be attributed the absolute or conditional reconfirmatoin of some of the converts from heresy,[23] and not to a defect of essential power on the part of the bishop who had confirmed them in heresy or schism. There can be no other explanation, since every validly consecrated bishop is of necessity capable of confirming validly. His episcopal character is a guarantee of his power in this matter.

At this point another dogmatic question calls for investigation, namely, what essentially differentiates the ordinary minister from the extraordinary minister of Confirmation; or, in other words, in what does the episcopal character differ from the priestly character. Besides the interest which this question assumes at this point, its prior discussion will help to solve *"une question subtile de metaphysique religieuse"*;[24] that is, what is the nature of the faculty which a simple priest receives to enable him to administer confirmation?

A summary of the teaching on the difficult problem of the nature of the episcopate may be found in either of two excellent articles recently published in the Australasian Catholic Record,[25] and in the American Ecclesiastical Review[26] respectively. In these articles it is shown that the vast majority of scholastic theologians denied the episcopate to be a distinct sacrament or order, and considered it only an extension of the priesthood.

Hugh of St. Victor, whose influence was admittedly great, though it was surpassed by that of his student Peter Lombard, distinguished different *dignities* in the *sacerdotium,* and asserted that the first dignity added to the priesthood was that of episcopate, the *princeps sacerdotium.*[27]

[23] Cf. Chap. II, Art. 3.

[24] D'Ales, *Bapteme et confirmation* (Paris: Bloud et Gay, 1928), p. 161.

[25] Roberts, "Episcopate and Presbyterate," *ACR,* IX (1932), 316-331.

[26] Connell, "The Episcopate," *ER,* LXXII (1925), 337-345.

[27] Cf. *ACR,* ibidem, p. 324.

Peter Lombard, and nearly all the commentators on the *Sententiae* up to the time of St. Robert Bellarmine (d. 1621), taught that the episcopate was not a distinct sacrament or order.[28]

Amongst the proponents of the extension theory there was a difference of opinion. According to the one group there was an internal extension of the priestly character: according to another the extension was only external. The former held that the priestly character was intrinsically affected by the episcopal consecration, the latter that the priestly character remained intrinsically unaltered, but was externally extended to include certain powers not possessed by a simple priest.[29]

Rightly understood neither opinion compromises episcopal superiority, for the superiority of the bishop with regard to orders and jurisdiction is clearly recognized.[30] But eventually the extension theory in both its forms lost its popularity.

St. Robert Bellarmine seriously questioned the view that had previously prevailed.[31] Then, mainly through his large influence, the tide of theological opinion was turned; and the episcopate was generally considered a distinct character. The Council of Trent was believed to favor Bellarmine's opinion.[32] In modern times it is definitely in the ascendancy.[33] So far the Church has left the nature of the episcopate undefined. There is sufficient doctrinal freedom to allow one to espouse any one of the theories presented.[34] In reference to confirmation, therefore, one may hold that the bishop is the ordinary minister by reason of a mere extension, intrinsic or extrinsic, of the priestly character; or one may maintain that the bishop owes his power to a distinct new sacrament received at his consecration.

After it has been seen that a bishop's "innate" power to confirm cannot be taken away in any circumstances, it is natural to

[28] Cf. ER, *ibidem,* pp. 340 ff.

[29] Cf. ER, *ibidem,* pp. 339-240.

[30] Cf. St. Thomas, *in Lib. IV Sententiarum,* Dist. XXIV, q. 2.

[31] Cf. ACR, *ibidem,* p. 324.

[32] ER, *ibidem,* p. 341.

[33] *Loc. cit.*

[34] Benedictus XIV, ep. *"In Postremo,"* 20 oct. 1756, § 17—*Fontes,* n. 442.

enquire whether in the absence of the present ecclesiastical prohibition, he could delegate that power to a simple priest. In view of the reservation of the faculty of delegating to the Pope it is certain that a bishop cannot now give this delegation.[35] the question prescinds, therefore, from any positive restrictions; and since the act of delegating a priest to confirm is regarded as an exercise of jurisdiction,[36] the investigation is restricted to bishops having jurisdiction. Owing to the present law which gives the Pope exclusive competence in this matter, it must be confessed that the point raised here is of little more than theoretical interest, as may be inferred from the incidental fashion in which writers are wont to touch upon it.

Some authorities have held that a bishop could delegate a priest to confirm were he not restrained from doing so by the sovereign Pontiff.[37] Various arguments are produced in favor of this opinion. It is contended that as a matter of fact bishops have on different occasions delegated priests to confirm.[38] The twentieth canon of the I Council of Toledo (403) has, as explained above,[39] been commonly understood as having granted to the priests authority to administer confirmation. This authority or delegation, it is assumed, came from the assembled bishops as from its ultimate source. In the same manner the delegation believed to have been given to priests by other particular councils[40] is regarded as coming from bishops acting in their ordinary official capacity.

Again, it is pointed out that it would be hard to assume that either Innocent I (402-417) or Gelasius I (492-496) would have given even tacit authorization to Greek priests to administer confirmation,[41] whereas it is known that the Greek priests were administering confirmation during the reigns of these illustrious

35 Cf. Benedictus XIV, *De Synodo Dioecesana,* Lib. VII, cap 8, n. 7.
36 Cappello, *De Sacramentis,* I, n. 205.
37 Cf. Benedictus XIV, *De Synodo Dioecesana,* Lib. VII, cap. 8, n. 3.
38 Cf. Benedictus XIV, *loc. cit.*
39 Chap. I, Art. 2.
40 *Ibidem.*
41 Cf. O'Dwyre, Confirmation, p. 172.

pontiffs.[42] Because of the known opposition of Innocent and Gelasius to priests confirming, it has been inferred that the faculty enjoyed by the Eastern priests of that period was received from their own bishops.

Besides, it has been maintained that with regard to his own diocese a bishop enjoys the same jurisdiction as the Pope enjoys over the universal Church; and, therefore, as a residential bishop he should share the papal authority of delegating priests to confirm.[43]

The arguments for the positive opinion cannot be conclusively set aside, as may be judged from the scholars who have adhered to it.[44] However, those who held that the power to delegate a priest to confirm belongs of its very nature to the Pope alone can present reasons which are certainly not less cogent than the reasons supporting the other opinion.

They maintain that it is by no means certain that the councils cited actually gave priests the power to confirm; but that it was more likely the power to perform a reconciliation ceremony.[45] Even if it be conceded that the bishops in session at the aforementioned councils did give priests the faculty of confirming in certain circumstances, it does not necessarily follow that in doing so they were acting purely on their own authority. The tacit consent would have been quite compatible with the prevailing law proclaimed so forcibly by Innocent and Gelasius.[46]

These Pontiffs' ruling was couched in general terms. It does not seem to have been more absolute than the ruling set forth later by Gregory I (590-603) for the priests of Lucania.[47] Still, the latter Pope in view of extraordinary circumstances allowed

[42] Cf. *Commentaria in Epist. ad Ephesios—MPG,* XVIII, 388; *Quest. in Nov. et Vet. Test.—MPG,* XV, 232.

[43] Verani, *Juris Canonicis Universi Commentarius* (3 vols., Monachii, 1903), Tom. I, Tit. XV, *De Sacra Unctione,* paragraph II, n. 20.

[44] Cf. Lehmkuhl, *Theologia Moralis,* II, 79; Cappello, *op. cit.,* I, n. 205; Benedict XIV, *De Synodo Dioecesana,* Lib. VII, cap. 8, n. 3.

[45] Cf. *Dictionaire de Theologie Catholique,* s.v. "Confirmation."

[46] Cf. Lehmkuhl, *op. cit.,* I, 79.

[47] *Ep. IX—MPL,* LXXVII, 675.

the bishops of Lucania to designate priests to confirm. Nor can Gregory be charged with any inconsistency. For the same reason it would not have been inconsistent or incompatible if bishops assembled at councils in the time of Innocent and Gelasius had a tacit papal permission to delegate priests for emergency cases.

In reference to the Eastern practice according to which priests confirmed at, and long before, the time of Gregory, it is not necessary to suppose that this was done without the knowledge of or contrary to the will of the Supreme Pontiff. In Gregory's second letter to Januarius he said: "In forbidding your priests to confirm we were acting in conformity with the ancient usage of *our* Church."[48] The Pope was therefore aware of a practice other than that followed in the Western Church; and the fact that he allowed this practice to continue indicates that it had at least his tacit consent; in other words, the Eastern bishops authorized priests to confirm only with the consent of the Holy Father.

At a later time documents emanated from Rome which seemed to assume that it was *only* by the consent of the Holy See that Eastern priests had the power to confirm. Whether this consent was express or only tacit does not matter as far as its essential effect is concerned.[49] In a letter which Clement VI (1342-1352) submitted to Consolator, Patriarch of the Armenians, occur two questions which have a very important bearing on the question now under discussion. The significance of these questions is enhanced by the fact that they were intended to probe the faith or ensure the orthodoxy of the suspect Patriarch. The questions were: 1. "Do you believe that it is only through the Roman Pontiff who has the plentitude of power that a dispensation to administer the sacrament of confirmation can be given to priests . . . ?" 2. Do you believe that those confirmed by priests who have not received for this a commission or some concession from the Roman Pontiff are to be again confirmed by a bishop?"[50]

[48] *Ep. XXVI—MPL,* LXXVII, 696.

[49] Cf. Deslandes, "Le Pretre Oriental Ministre de la Confirmation," *Echos d'Orient,* XXIX (1930), 11.

[50] Denzinger, *Enchiridion,* nn. 573-574.

In the first question Clement apparently assumes that it is by his plentitude of power that the Roman Pontiff delegates a simple priest to confirm: that is it by reason of a power which is peculiar to him as Pope, and which therefore no bishop possesses by reason of his office or jurisdiction. The second question goes further, because it insinuates that confirmation administered by a simple priest was invalid, unless he had delegation from the Roman Pontiff, directly or indirectly, expressly or tacitly. The force of these questions becomes more apparent when it is realized that at the time they were formulated confirmation was being administered by priests in the East, and had been administered by them for perhaps nine hundred years before. Consolator was presumably acquainted with the history of the administration of confirmation by priests in the East; and now he is asked two questions the implications of which he cannot evade.[51]

In the lights of these questions or their implication it seems hard to concede that the Eastern bishops, or any other bishops, ever possessed in virtue of their jurisdiction the faculty of delegating priests to confirm. Nor, in spite of the absence of any authentic record, is their any great difficulty attached to the claim that the Eastern priests received their authority to confirm from the Pope.

In this connection a distinction is to be made between obtaining a faculty by an express and formal grant, and obtaining it by a tacit or *legal* concession.[52] It is by the latter method, according to all authorities, that the Greek priests have obtained the faculty to confirm.

An Instruction of Benedict XIV to the Copts favors the tacit or legal concession theory. He said: "By a certain kindness and sufferance on the part of the Holy See it has happened that both sacraments (baptism and confirmation) have been administered among the Greeks in the Orient by the same priests, and there are theologians who hold that this toleration (of the Holy See) has the character of a tacit dispensation.

[51] Cf. Deslandes, *ibidem*, p. 12.

[52] Cf. Lehmkuhl, *op. cit.*, I, p. 79.

It is worthy of note that the *Decretum pro Armenis* as contained in the Bull *Exultate Deo* issued by Pope Eugene IV under date of November 22, 1439, in its implicit admission of a priest's ability to confirm, says that he had been doing so by delegation of the *Apostolic See.*[53] Though the Council of Florence was charged with trying to effect a reunion of the East and West, and to that end the Holy See was particularly conciliatory towards the Greeks, yet the Decree which was issued in the Council by authority of Eugent IV would not concede that confirmation had been administered by priests delegated by any other authority than the Apostolic See.

In reference to the other argument given in favor of the bishop's power to delegate, it must be said that it has no validity. A bishop has not the same authority in his own diocese as the Pope has over the universal Church. Christ has entrusted the Pope with the government of the entire Church. Therefore his very position demands power and authority not required in the administration of a diocese.[54]

In terminating the discussion as to whether or not a bishop could *ex natura rei* delegate a priest to confirm, it must be conceded that the positive opinion has some probability, but in the light of the evidence adduced it seems much more probable that a bishop is without the inherent power necessary to delegate a simple priest to administer the sacrament of confirmation.

As already indicated, there is no doubt that a bishop can be commissioned to delegate a priest to administer confirmation. Even a priest, it will be seen, can be delegated by the Holy See to communicate the faculty of confirming to another priest. In the Code of Canon Law, however, neither the bishop nor the priest is given this power.

But neither does the Code *expressly* forbid bishops or others who have the faculty of confirming to delegate the faculty. The law does say that the power of orders which has been attached

[53] Cf. Denzinger, *Enchiridion*, n. 697.

[54] Cf. Verani, *op. cit.*, Tom. I, Tit. XV, *De Sacra Unctione*, paragraph II, n. 20.

to an office or committed to a person by a legitimate ecclesiastical superior cannot be delegated to others, unless the law or an indult explicitly allows such delegation;[55] and some canonists give the delegation of a priest to confirm as an instance of what is forbidden by the Code.[56] When however a priest is delegated to confirm he is not given a power of orders. That point is well established.[57] Therefore the canon cited must be understood as having no reference to the delegation of a priest for confirmation.

Though the common law gives no bishop or other ordinary the faculty to delegate priests to confirm, particular law and apostolic indults frequently give this faculty to ordinaries in missionary countries. Thus a bishop of Conception, Chile, where missionary conditions exist up to this day[58] was given the faculty to delegate one or two priests as necessity required.[59] At present all the bishops of Latin America, but not their vicars general, have authority to delegate priests to give confirmation.[60] In territory subject to the Congregation for the Propagation of the Faith ordinaries are given the "Power to give to one or two of their priests the faculty of administering the sacrament of confirmation in places remote from their (ordinaries') residence, provided however that in such places no bishop is available."[61]

This faculty of ordinaries in missionary countries is not limited by stringent regulations which affect its valid use. Thus when the faculty reads: "to delegate one or two priests", it does not mean that the ordinary can delegate *only* one or two. Because this

[55] Canon 310.

[56] Cf. Blat, *Commentarium,* II, n. 159; Woywod, *A Practical Commentary on the Code of Canon Law* (2 vols., 4. ed., New York: Joseph Wagner, 1932), I, 363.

[57] This particular subject will be considered in Chapter IV, Art. 3.

[58] Cf. Zerba, "Instructio pro Simplice Sacerdote sacramentum Confirmationis ex Sedis Apostolicae Delegatione Administranti," *Apollinaris,* VIII (1935), 41-46.

[59] S.C. de Prop. Fide, 24 iul. 1841—*Coll. S.C.P.F.,* n. 933.

[60] Sacra Congregatio Consistorialis, 28 apr. 1939—*AAS,* XXXI (1939), 224.

[61] Vermeersch-Creusen, *Epitome,* I, n. 873, Formula Tertia Maior, (A) n. 3.

is an extraordinary concession in the Latin Church the number delegated should be small;[62] yet, account is to be taken of the size and population of the particular missionary territory subject to the ordinary.[63] The clause limiting the delegation of priests for places situated far from the ordinary's residence is to be taken in a moral sense: that is, the difficulty of travel, the age of strength of the ordinary must be taken into consideration.[64] Neither is the phrase which says that the priest is given a faculty to be exercised when no bishop is available to be taken too strictly. It is understood to mean: "when no bishop is present who is able and willing to confirm as frequently and opportunely as the people require it".[65]

With regard to the interpretation of faculties of this kind it must be remembered that the Church does not wish to have the faithful of missionary countries in a less advantageous position than the faithful in a well organized ecclesiastical territory: quite the contrary contains.[66] Hence all the clauses attached to the ordinary's faculty to delegate a priest to confirm in missionary countries have to do with the lawful, not the valid, use of this faculty.[67]

From what has been written on paragraph 1 of canon 782 it is sufficiently clear what the law means when it says: "the bishop alone is the ordinary minister of confirmation". The unique position of the bishop has been definitely stated: and in the realms of theology and canon law it has been clearly established. No question of much practical importance on the ordinary minister is in dispute at the present day; though of course the theorists have still a number of questions on which they may exercise their spe-

[62] Cf. Canon 19.

[63] Cf. Vromant, *Facultates Apostolicae quas S.C. de Prop. Fide delegare solet Ordinariis Missionum Commentaria in Formulam Tertiam* (Lovanii: Editions du Museum Lessianum, 1926), p. 28. For this work the abbreviation, "Commentaris in Formulam Tertiam" will be used.

[64] Cf. Vromant, *loc. cit.*

[65] Cf. Vromant, *loc. cit.*

[66] Cf. Iglesias, apud Vromant, *loc. cit.*

[67] Cf. Vermeersch, *Periodica*, XI (1931), (14).

culative ingenuity. Passing then from the defined dogmatic question, and the less practical aspects of the first part of the canon, one must examine the rules that are to guide the bishop in the exercise of his power as a minister of confirmation.

Article 3. Bishop Confirming in His Own Diocese

Canon 783, § 1: *Episcopus in sua dioecesi hoc sacramentum confirmationis etiam extraneis legitime ministrat, nisi obstet expressa proprii eorum Ordinarii prohibitio.*

The Code gives the bishop a maximum of freedom with regard to the persons he may confirm. There is of course no question about his own subjects in his own diocese. But within his own territory he is permittted to confirm in addition to these the subjects of other ordinaries, unless these latter have issued an express prohibition. The "strangers" or non-subjects whom the Code allows the bishop to confirm under the circumstances laid down in canon 783, § 1, are those who do not possess a domicile or quasi-domicile in his territory, and are not in the position of *vagi.*[68]

The bishop has not always enjoyed this amount of freedom regarding the subject of confirmation. The Sacred Congregation of the Council declared in 1602 that it was not lawful for a bishop to administer confirmation to non-subjects without the permission of their ordinary.[69]

Writers prior to Barbosa (d. 1649) maintained that a bishop needed express permission before he could confirm the subjects of other ordinaries even in his own diocese; and, besides, they contended that a bishop acting without this permission incurred suspension from the exercise of pontificals.[70] Barbosa himself rejected the opinion that a bishop was liable to this *latae sententiae* penalty, and asserted that with reasonably presumed permission

[68] Cf. Canons 91-95; Blat, *Commentarium,* III, Pars. I, n. 77.

[69] Pallottini, *Collectio omnium Conclusionum et Resolutionum Quae in causis propositis apud Sacram Congregationem Cardinalium S. Concilii Tridentini interpretum Prodieurunt* (18 vols., Romae, 1862-1895), XVI, p. 28, n. 11.

[70] Cf. Barbosa, *Juris Eccles. Universi Libri III,* Lib. I, cap. 2, n. 47.

a bishop in his own diocese might confirm the subjects of another ordinary.[71] La Croix (d. 1714) likewise insisted that reasonably presumed consent was sufficient for the bishop in this case; but he regarded it as a grave sin for the bishop to act without this presumed consent.[72] Ferraris (d. ca. 1763) in his day taught the same thing;[73] and so it developed that consent might nearly always be presumed; or it happened that in certain places custom permitted the bishop to confirm strangers in his diocese.[74]

Under the present law it is taken for granted that no bishop has any objection to some of his subjects being confirmed outside the diocese by another bishop. So strong is this presumption that a bishop who does object is required to issue an express prohibition, before his desires have to be respected.[75] If, then, a bishop confirming in his own diocese is approached by the subjects of a neighboring ordinary, he may confirm them, though there are indications that the neighboring ordinary is opposed. At least the Code does not require him to abstain from confirming such people. Nor does it require him to refrain from confirming when there is an implicit or interpretative prohibition. The strict law permits him to confirm, provided only there is no express veto.[76]

If, to take an improbable instance, an ordinary should whimsically issue a prohibition of this kind, a neighboring bishop would have to abide by it, and could not lawfully act in opposition to it.[77] At least in the hypothesis that has been made, that

[71] Cf. Barbosa, *loc. cit.*

[72] *Theologia Moralis* (3 vols., Coloniae, 1779), Tom. II, Lib. VI, cap. 2, Dubium 2, n. 1.

[73] *Prompta Bibliotheca Canonica* (9 vols., Romae, 1885-1899), s.v. "Confirmatio," n. 10.

[74] Cf. Layman, *Theologia Moralis* (2 vols., Patavii, 1733), Lib. V, Tract. III, Cap. VI, n. 2; Kenrick, *Theologia Moralis,* (3 vols., Baltimore, 1866). II, 124.

[75] Cf. Ayrinhac, *Legislation on the Sacraments in the New Code of Canon Law* (New York: Longmans, Green and Co., 1928), *Confirmation,* n. 52.

[76] Cf. Blat, *Commentarium,* Lib. III, Pars I, n. 77.

[77] Cf. Blat, *loc. cit.*

would be the general rule, lest there should be occasion for discord or scandal.

Seeing on the other hand the Church's desire to give the faithful every reasonable facility to receive confirmation,[78] and realizing the great benefit conferred by this sacrament,[79] one fails to comprehend how in any instance a purely arbitrary restriction should stand against the Church's wish, or against the timely conferring of an important spiritual aid on one or more members of the faithful.

But can an ordinary *reasonably* forbid his subject to receive confirmation from a bishop in another diocese? The Code seems to assume that he can. Commentators are noticeably silent on the point. An answer then can only be suggested.

In relation to his subjects a bishop is like the paternal head of a household.[80] He is united to them by bonds of fatherly affection and pastoral solicitude; and they in humble submission look to him to provide for their spiritual needs.[81]

Another reason also comes to mind. The bishop's visit to a parish for the purpose of administering confirmation is a very important parochial event. It is an occasion when he has an opportunity of speaking directly and personally to his people, many of whom will not see or hear him until he has to come around again for confirmation. It is important, therefore, that the occasion be attended with all possible ceremony and solemnity,[82] and that there be a large attendance of parishioners, particularly of the relatives of the *confirmandi*. It goes without saying that a large class of candidates lends impressiveness to the event. But this ideal would be to a large extent frustrated, if a week or two before the bishop's arrival a large percentage of the people had gone across the diocesan boundary line to receive confirmation from another bishop in another diocese, simply because there was

[78] Cf. canon 785.

[79] Cf. *Cathechismus Concilii Tridentini* (Romae, 1886), Cap. III, n. 20.

[80] Cf. I Timothy, III, 5.

[81] Cf. I Corinthians, IV, 1.

[82] Cf. *Pontificale Romanum, Ordo ad Visitandas Parochias.*

some particular attraction in this latter place. That, then, is another instance where a bishop might legitimately forbid his subjects to go into another diocese for confirmation; and such prohibition should be recognized by neighboring bishops. Knowing the relations that properly exist between a bishop and his flock, surely there is no one who cannot see that these necessary relations are preserved and perfected, when the faithful are confirmed by their own bishop, and the bishop confirms his own subjects, giving them strength and fortitude for the battle which they must wage under his leadership. Therefore it seems that normally the people should be confirmed by their own bishop; and to insure the general observance of this rule it might be necessary for the bishop of a particular locality to *insist* on his subjects' coming to him for confirmation. In a particular diocese or locality, then, a bishop might legitimatley *forbid* his subject to go outside the diocese for confirmation.

Like the pre-Code authorities,[83] commentators of the present day also teach that it would be *gravely* illegal for a bishop in his diocese to confirm strangers against the express prohibition of their proper ordinary.[84] It seems to be presumed by the commentators that the prohibition of the stranger's ordinary is not manifestly unreasonable, and that there is nothing extraordinary to prevent the confirmation of strangers being deferred until their own bishop can minister to them. Only with this presumption obtaining can a bishop who confirms in his diocese against the express command of their own ordinary be accused of grave sin.

The "ordinary" who in certain circumstances may forbid his subjects to be confirmed by a bishop outside the diocese is in no instance a major superior of an exempt clerical religious institute for though these are ordinaries[85] they have no subjects who might

[83] Cf. La Croix, *Theologia Moralis,* Tom. II, VI, Cap. II, Dubium II, n. 1; Vermeersch, *Theologia Moralis* (3 vols., 3. ed., Romae: Universitas Gregoriana, 1926-1928), III, n. 206; Lehmkuhl, *Theologia Moralis,* II, n. 142.

[84] Cf. Cappello, *De Sacramentis,* I, n. 201; Merkelbach, *Summa Theologiae Moralis* (3 vols., Romae: Marietti, 1927), III, n. 186.

[85] Canon 198.

be candidates for confirmation.[86] He is therefore a local ordinary. From the nature of the case it may be a residential bishop, an abbot or prelate *nullius*,[87] an apostolic administrator permanently constituted,[88] or a vicar or prefect apostolic.[89] It does not seem that of himself the vicar general may issue the prohibition in question, for though he is a local ordinary[90] and has authority to give precepts[91] he would probably require a special mandate to issue this order;[92] or at least it would be a matter that should be referred to the bishop.[93] With regard to the other local ordinaries who may temporarily rule a vacant diocese or similar territory,[94] it appears that for a special reason they could forbid their subjects to be confirmed by a bishop outside the diocese. If a sufficient reason for such a prohibition existed, these temporary ordinaries could hardly be accused of innovation, *sede vacante*.[95]

Canon 783, § 1, which is under discussion, allows the bishop *in his own diocese* to confirm his own subjects and, with the proviso therein stated, also non-subjects.

Certain exempt religious once sought to deny the bishop's right to confirm in their churches, parochial and non-parochial. Benedict XIV with a mild rebuke to the effect that these religious were far too much concerned about their privileges of exemption affirmed that the bishop had a right to confirm in these churches at or outside the time of visitation.[96] Long before that the Sacred Congregation of the Council had declared that the bishop might confirm in the parish church of exempt religious "*invitis ipsis regularibus*", and that he could inflict censures on regulars who tried to prevent him.[97]

[86] Cf. Canon 544, § 1.
[87] Cf. Canons 198, 323.
[88] Cf. Canons 198, 315, § 1.
[89] Cf. Canon 198, 294.
[90] Canon 198.
[91] Cf. Cicognani, *Canon Law*, p. 634.
[92] Cf. Vermeersch-Creusen, *Epitome Iuris Canonici*, I, n. 479.
[93] Cf. Canon 369.
[94] Cf. Canons 198, 431, 432, 309, 327, § 1.
[95] Cf. Canon 436.
[96] Const. "*Firmandus*," 6 nov. 1744, § 6—*Fontes*, n. 349.
[97] S.C.C., *Brixien*, 9 iul. 1657—*Fontes*, n. 2750.

At the present time the Code itself defines the bishop's right to confirm subjects or non-subjects *anywhere* in the diocese: "The Bishop has the right to administer confirmation *also* in exempt places within the confines of the territory of his diocese."[98]

A little mutual good-will and consideration on the part of the bishop and religious would prevent any undue inconvenience or embarrassment to either in the exercise of their respective rights. This refers particularly to the time at which confirmation should be administered in exempt places.[99]

Regarding a bishop confirming in his own diocese there is one more point which may very easily be overlooked, but which is of such importance that it is the subject of a distinct canon in the Code of Canon Law. If the bishop confirms any people whose pastor is not present at the ceremony, then the bishop must inform the pastor of these people about their confirmation. It is not necessary that the bishop perform this duty personally. He may have some other one do it. In either case the bishop must discharge the obligation as soon as possible.[99a]

ARTICLE 4. BISHOP CONFIRMING IN ANOTHER DIOCESE

Canon 783, § 2: *In aliena diocesi indiget licentia Ordinarii loci saltem rationabilter praesumpta, nisi agatur de propriis subditis quibus confirmation conferat privatim ac sine baculo et mitra.*

Paragraph 2 of canon 783 is but another indication of the legislator's respect for the rights of the ordinary within his proper territory.[100] It will not permit a bishop to administer confirmation in another bishop's diocese without regard for the will of the local ordinary, unless there is question of the bishop's own subjects,[101] and the circumstances warrant private administration. There must be reasonably presumed permission before the bishop may confirm any people whatsoever solemnly, or non-subjects privately, in another diocese.[102]

98 Canon 792.

99 Cf. Canon 415, § 4.

99a Canon 799.

100 Cf. Canons 337, 1337, 1637.

101 Cf. p.

102 Cf. Cappello, De Sacramentis, I, n. 201.

The Old Law was much more strict. Prior to the Code a bishop who confirmed in the diocese of another without the latter's express consent, *ipso facto* incurred suspension from the exercise of pontificals.[103] This applied also to a metropolitan in relation to his suffragan sees,[104] particularly because he did not enjoy, as now the metropolitan does,[105] the right of exercising pontificals in every church of his suffragan sees.[106]

The decree of the Council of Trent which authors[107] cite as proof that the bishop incurred suspension for confirming without express permission in another's diocese is directly concerned with the exercise of pontificals in another's diocese. Certainly, therefore, the penalty of suspension was incurred for the solemn administration of confirmation. Would it have been incurred also for the private administration of confirmation in another diocese without due permission? The writers make no distinction; they simply state that suspension from the exercise of pontificals was inurred *eo ipso* for confirming in the diocese of another ordinary without his express permission.[108] Why a distinction was not made is hard to understand, for the rules of interpretation could hardly have permitted the extension of a penalty for the unlawful use of pontificals to a case where pontificals were not actually exercised.[109] Perhaps the private administration of confirmation in another diocese was considered so unusual that it did not merit discussion in what after all did not pretend to be more than general treatises on confirmation.

At the present time the point is only of historical interest, for

103 "Nulli episcopo liceat, cuiusvis privilegii praetextu pontificalia in alterius dioecesi exercere, nisi de Ordinarii loci expressa licentia, et in personas eidem Ordinario subjectas tantum; si secus factum fuerit, episcopus ab exercitio pontificalium, et sic ordinati ab executione ordinum sint ipso jure suspensi."—Conc. Trident., sess. VI, *de ref.*, c. 4.

104 Cf. Ferraris, *Biblotheca, s.v.* "Confirmatio," n. 9.

105 Canon 274, 6°.

106 Cf. Ferraris, *Bibliotheca,* s.v. *"Confirmatio,"* n. 10.

107 Barbosa, *Juris Eccles. Universi Libri III,* Lib. I, cap. 2, n. 46.

108 Cf. Barbosa, Ferraris, *loc. cit.*

109 *In poenis benignior est interpretatio facienda*—Reg. 49, R. J., in VI°.

the Code has no penalty for contravening the prescript of canon 783. The former penalty is abrogated, because one of the *normae generales* of the Code says: "With regard to penalties of which there is no mention in the Code, whether they be spiritual or temporal, medicinal or so-called vindictive, *latae* or *ferendae sententia,* they are to be considered abrogated." [110]

Apparently the Council of Trent found it necessary to take severe measures for the removal of a serious prevalent abuse.[111] Subsequent to the successful eradication of this abuse, the Code did not have any need to retain the rigid regulation made for another era. It therefore furnished a law which is without a sanction, but which provides a sufficient safeguard for the rights of each ordinary in his own diocese, and at the same time allows an exception that may be found very convenient in particular cases.

By the phrase "in another diocese" must be understood not only a diocese in the strict sense,[112] but also similar territorial divisions such as abbacies and prelacies *nullius,*[113] vicariates and prefectures apostolic.[114] Even with regard to the two latter cases, in which there is usually much to be desired in the way of church organization and spiritual opportunities for the faithful, the Code does not give an extern bishop any right to interfere. The spiritual affairs of these territories are subject to the authority of the vicar and prefect apostolic.[115] So has the Code ordained.

By particular law, however, there may be some exceptions in view of the particular conditions of missionary regions. In the faculties which are usually granted to ordinaries in missionary countries is included the power of delegating one or two priest to administer confirmation in any place that is remote from the ordinary's residence, provided that no bishop be available in that

[110] Canon 6, 5°.

[111] Note the strict wording of the prohibition as contained in footnote 98, *supra.*

[112] Cf. Vermeersch-Creusen, *Epitome,* I, n. 329.

[113] Canon 215.

[114] Cf. canon 294, § 1.

[115] Cf. canons 294-308.

place.[116] It would seem that if a bishop happens to be passing through or staying temporarily in a place far away from the ordinary's residence in such a missionary country, he hardly need concern himself about having the reasonably presumed consent of the local ordinary. In such circumstances the required permission seems to be implicitly given by the Holy See.

"Reasonably presumed permission" is had when in view of the particular circumstances it may be conjectured that had the permission been sought it would have been granted.[117] A bishop might have one of many reasons for presuming the local ordinary's permission to administer confirmation solemnly. It might be that the particular local ordinary had been in the habit of inviting him to confirm in a certain part of the diocese; or that because of the advanced age or poor health of the local ordinary it would be very acceptable to him to have confirmation administered by one of his intimate brethren in the hierarchy.

Permission to administer confirmation privately to non-subjects in another diocese might be more readily presumed, because when the private administration of the sacrament is permitted there is usually some emergency, or urgency.[118] The case is frequently that of an unconfirmed person being found in danger of death. The practice in Rome, where it is the custom to call in any bishop to confirm an infant who is in danger of death, is in complete conformity with this opinion.[119]

No permission, actual or presumed, is required if a bishop wants to confirm his own subjects privately and without mitre and crosier in the diocese of another ordinary. When a reasonable cause permits the private administration of confirmation[120] a bishop need not have any hesitation about confirming his subjects

[116] Cf. "*Formulae Facultatum Quas S.C. de Prop. Fide Ordinariis in Terris Missionum Procurat,*" Vermeersch-Creusen, Epitome, Vol. I, Appendix II.

[117] Cf. Blat, *Commentarium,* Lib. III, Pars I, n. 77.

[118] Cf. infra, footnote 120.

[119] Vermeersch-Creusen, *Epitome,* II, n. 66.

[120] S.C.S. Off., (Coreae), 12 febr. 1851, ad I—*Fontes,* n. 915; S.C. de Prop. Fide (Bosniae), 6 dec. 1626—*Collectanea,* n. 29.

outside his own diocese. He might easily have occasion to use this faculty in a hospital or similar instiution of another diocese.

By "private administration" is understood administration in a place which is not a church or public or semi-public oratory; for instance, in a private home, or hospital room.[121] For any just reason the bishop may confirm without mitre and crosier, using only the rochetto and stole, or even without the rochetto, using only the stole.[122]

Like the pre-Code law, the law of the Code does not give the Metropolitan any more right to confirm in a suffragan see than a suffragan bishop has to confirm in another diocese,[123] though the metropolitan is at present otherwise free to exercise pontificals in the other dioceses of his province.[124] Neither is the administration of confirmation listed amongst the acts he may perform when, for a just reason approved by the Holy See, he makes the visitation of the diocese of a negligent suffragan bishop.[125] It is quite probable that in making this visitation upon request of the Holy See he would have instructions to administer confirmation at the same time.[126]

The analysis of canon 783, and its comparison with pre-Code law, shows that "the limits of lawful administration have been extended in the bishop's favor." No doubt the comparative freedom which the bishop now enjoys will also be for the convenience of some of the candidates for confirmation. The new legislation on the points in question is therefore superior to the old.

An observation made at the conclusion of the previous article applies here also. When the bishop confirms people whose proper pastor is not present at the administration of the sacrament, the

[121] Cf. Blat, *Commentarium*, Lib. III, Pars I, n. 77.

[122] Cf. Cappello, *De Sacramentis*, I, n. 213.

[123] Cf. Augustine, *A Commentary on Canon Law* (8 vols., St. Louis: B. Herder, 1921-1929), Vol. IV, (3. 4d., 1925), III.

[124] Canon 274, 6°.

[125] Cf. canon 274, 5°.

[126] Augustine, Commentary, IV, III.

information necessary for the records of the proper pastor must be forwarded to him without delay.[126a]

Article 5. The Bishop's Obligation to Confirm

Canon 785, §1: *Episcopus obligatione tenetur sacramentum hoc subditis rite et rationabiliter petentibus conferendi, praesertim tempore visitationis dioecesis.*

The residential bishop is a pastor of souls in the diocese committed to him.[127] As a pastor he is bound *sub gravi* and *ex justitia* to administer the sacraments or have them administered to his subjects who reasonably ask for them.[128] He is under this obligation by reason of his office, not only when there is question of the spiritual necessity of his people, but also when it is only a matter of their spiritual profit or utility.[129] In consideration, then, of the spiritual strength and fortitude of which the sacrament of confirmation is a perennial source,[130] it is evident that as chief diocesan pastor the bishop is bound to give his people an opportunity and a facility for the reception of this sacrament.

Long before the bishop's obligation "was so clearly and severely defined" because it was long before the Code, Suarez (d. 1617) argued that the bishop by reason of his pastoral office had a grave obligation to administer confirmation to his subjects at opportune times. According to this *Jesuit luminary*, who had a vivid sense of the virtue of confirmation, this obligation rests upon the bishop, because as a shepherd he is bound to minister unto his flock, not only with regard to what is nceessary for salvation, but also with regard to the things which have been instituted by Christ for the *benefit* of the Church and its individual members, and which therefore can be justly expected and demanded by the faithful.[131]

[126a] Canon 799.

[127] Canon 334.

[128] Vermeersch, *Theologia Moralis* (3 vols., 2. ed., Romae: Universitas Gregoriana, 1926-1927), Vol. III, n. 181.

[129] Cf. Cappello, *De Sacramentis,* Vol. I, n. 67.

[130] Cf. *Concilii Plenarii Baltimorensis II, Acta et Decreta,* n. 247.

[131] *Opera Omnia* (26 .vols., Parisiis: 1856-1861), Vol. XX, Quaes LXXII, Art. XII, Sectio II, n. 1.

But before the Code this obligation of the bishop was not interpreted so strictly as it now.[132]

It was then considered sufficient if a bishop gave the people of his diocese an opportunity of confirmation every nine or ten years,[133] or at least if the more important parts of the diocese had such an opportunity at intervals of nine or ten years.[134] Strange as it may seem particularly after the appearance of the Code, Bouix (d. 1870) had taught that there was no real obligation on the part of the bishop to administer confirmation.[135] That doctrine has been fortunately repudiated. Even to those who lack an appreciation of the importance of the sacrament of confirmation,[136] or who are unacquainted with the Church's undying concern for its timely administration to the faithful,[137] the opinion of Bouix is untenable after the promulgation of the Code. Besides, the common pre-Code interpretation of the bishop's obligation to confirm has been found much too lenient.[138]

In English the present law on the bishop's obligation reads: "The bishop is bound to administer confirmation to his subjects who legitimately and reasonably ask for it, especially at the time of the diocesan visitation." This prescript is understood to mean that the bishop has a grave obligation to furnish the candidates for confirmation in each part of his diocese a suitable opportunity of receiving it from time to time and at least once every five years.[139] There would be an obligation to give this opportunity to

[132] Cf. O'Donnell, "Confirmation in the New Code," *IER,* XI (1918), 211.

[133] Cf. Sabetti-Barrett, *Compendium Theologiae Moralis* (19. ed., Ratisbonae, 1906), *De Confirmatione,* n. 673.

[134] Cf. Genicot, *Theologiae Moralis Institutiones* (2 vols., Louvanii, 1886-1897), II, 162.

[135] *De Episcopo,* Vol. II, p. 313, Quaes. VI.

[136] Cf. *Catechismus Concilii Tridentini,* Cap. III, n. 20.

[137] Cf. c. 1, D. V, *de cons.;* c. 3, D. V, *de cons.;* Benedictus *XIV,* instr. *"Eo quamvis tempore,"* 4 maii 1745, § 8—*Fontes,* n. 357; Pius VI, ep. *"Cum sicut accepimus,"* 10 apr. 1775, § 2—*Fontes,* n. 468.

[138] Cf. O'Donnell, "Confirmation in the New Code," *IER,* XI (1918), 211.

[139] Cf. Pruemmer, *Manuale Iuris Canonici* (4-5. ed., Friburgi Brisgo-

the people of the more important parts of the diocese more frequently, if not annually.[140] All this however is from the point of view of *legal* obligation.

The bishop's pastoral instinct is not circumscribed by the limits of purely legal obligations. He is aware that after his young charges have reached the use of reason, and are being assailed by the forces of evil, they must not be left long without the protection which the sacrament of confirmation was designed to give.[141] In a non-Catholic country particularly he realizes the many dangers there are of children's losing their faith after they have attained the use of reason, and their "spiritual combat" has begun;[142] and therefore he hastens to bring them timely aid for their struggle by the early administration of the sacrament of confirmation.

Besides the general opportunities for confirmation which the bishop is obliged to afford his people, he is also required to administer confirmation to those who legitimately and reasonably ask for it. They are people who have the qualities requisite in the subject of confirmation,[143] who have a special reason for not being required to wait until a certain fixed time,[144] and who make their request in circumstances where they may be confirmed with propriety and without undue inconvenience to the bishop.[145]

A particular request of this kind would be very likely to come from a person about to be married. The law requires unconfirmed people contemplating marriage to receive confirmation before being admitted to matrimony, if they can do so without grave inconvenience.[146] "This obligation," says Cappello, "is at least in a

viae; Herder and Co., 1927), p. 377; Vermeersch-Creusen, *Epitome,* II, n. 64; Cappello, *De Sacramentis,* I, n. 207; Sipos, *Enchiridion Iuris Canonici* (Pecs, 1926), p. 430.

[140] Cf. Wernz-Vidal, *Ius Canonicum* (7 vols. in 8, Romae: Apud Aedes Universitatis Gregorianae, 1923-1938), Vol. IV. Pars I, n. 55.

[141] Cf. *Il Monitore Ecclesiastico,* V (1935), III.

[142] Cf. *Acta et Decreta Concilii Plenarii Baltimorensis* III, n. 14.

[143] Cf. Augustine, *Commentary,* IV, 110.

[144] Cf. canon 1021, § 2.

[145] Cf. Blat. *Commentarium,* Lib. III, Pars I, n. 79.

[146] Canon 1021, § 2.

wide sense based on the divine law."[147] Therefore unconfirmed people about to be married may legitimatley and reasonably ask the bishop to confirm them. In such an instance there would usually be a little inconvenience to the bishop, because in such particular cases he would be permitted to confirm privately, vested in rochet and stole.[148]

Another particular request which the bishop would be bound to accede to might be made by those unable for some reason to attend the common solemn confirmation ceremony in church. For example, soldiers or sailors in individual instances might find it necessary to approach a bishop privately in order to be confirmed. Any request of this kind which is not manifestly illegitimate or unreasonable, even an implicit request,[149] will receive a ready response from the bishop, who is aware of the special utility of confirmation in the *Christian* warfare and the urgent need of spiritual reenforcement in individual cases.

The obligation of the bishop to confirm those particular people who reasonably and legitimately ask for it is not considered grave, if it can rightly be supposed that his refusal will not cause any scandal. If the administration of the sacrament can be conveniently deferred until a future proximate occasion, the bishop is under no immediate obligation to administer it upon request.[150] If confirmation cannot reasonably be put off, the bishop is bound *sub leve* to confer it at once.[151]

A bishop who fulfills the general obligation of canon 785, § 1, by giving every part of his diocese the opportunities for confirmation which that canon requires, may be satisfying only the common law. He must look to particular legislation to see if he is bound by a more stringent legal obligation to give the people a chance of being confirmed.

[147] *De Sacramentis,* Vol. III, Pars I, n. 150.

[148] Cf. responses S.C. de Prop. Fide (Bosniae) 6 dec. 1626—*Collectanea,* n. 29; S.C.S. Off. (Coreae), 12 feb. 1851—*Collectanea,* n. 1057.

[149] Cf. Cappello, *De Sacramentis,* I, n. 67.

[150] Cf. Cappello, *De Sacramentis,* I, n. 207.

[151] Cf. Cappello, *loc. cit.*

In the United States conciliar law on this matter is more exacting. It requires the bishops "to visit their entire diocese *at least once every three years,*[152] not only that they may know their flock, and see with their own eyes what is necessary for the spiritual good of their people, but also that the faithful *who are exposed to so many dangers of losing their faith* in this country may be *fortified* by the sacrament of *confirmation.*"[153]

This legislation of the III Plenary Council of Baltimore (1884) has not been abrogated by the Code.[154]. It is still in force in this country.[155] Nor is it to be regarded lightly.

The great importance which the Council attached to giving the people of the whole diocese an opportunity for confirmation at least once in three years is signified by the duty enjoined on the bishop in the event that he is unable to fulfill his obligation of confirming personally. If he is personally unable to give the people of the diocese an opportunity of receiving confirmation at least once every three years, he is obliged to call upon a neighboring bishop for assistance, so that no part of the diocese may be denied the spiritual opportunity desired by the Fathers.[156] The emphasis which the American bishops put upon their regular and frequent administration of confirmation in all parts of the diocese is further indicated by the change of wording which was introduced when, at the III Plenary Council, Decree 86 of the previous Council was

[152] No italics in original text.

[153] " . . . Unusquisque igitur Episcopus saltem unoquoque triennio totam diocesim perlustrare teneatur, non solum ut gregem suum cognoscat eaque omnia quae ad spirituale eorum bonum necessaria sunt suis ipse oculis perspiciat, sed etiam ut fideles tot amittendae fidei in hac regione periculis expositos Sacramento Confirmationis munire possit . . . ."—*Acta et Decreta Concilii Plenarii Baltimorensis* III, n. 14.

[154] Cf. canon 22; Barrett, *A Comparative Study of the Councils of Baltimore and the Code of Canon Law* (The Catholic University of America, Canon Law Studies, n. 83, Washington, D. C.: The Catholic University of America, 1932), p. 67.

[155] Cf. Barrett, *op, cit., Appendix* I, n. 12.

[156] " . . . Quod si per se ipse facere nequeat, id per alios idoneos viros praestet, adhibito etiam pro Sacramento Confirmationis alicuius inter viciniores Episcopos ministerio . . . "—*Acta de Decreta,* n. 14.

substantially repeated. The II Council had said: "Bishops shall remember that they are strictly bound to visit their diocese regularly and frequently, not only that they may administer the sacrament of confirmation at stated times, but also that they may know their flock well . . ." By making a syntactical change in this decree, the III Council gave the clause *on administering confirmation* the emphatic position. Note the structure of N. 14: "Each bishop shall therefore visit his entire diocese at least every three years, not only that he may know his flock . . . *but also* that the faithful who are exposed to so many dangers of losing their faith in this country may be fortified by this sacrament . . ." The significance of this deliberate alternation need not be stressed.

These are some of the wise provisions which the vigilant Fathers of Baltimore made for the preservation of the faith in this country. Their importance as well as their binding force endures to the present day. Rightly therefore do the bishops of this country have so much regard for them.

There has been little difficulty about defining the bishop's general obligations as imposed by the common law and the III Plenary Council of Baltimore. There remain particular questions regarding which there is not so much agreement among the canonists and moralists. Points are raised respecting the confirmation of a dying person petitioning to be confirmed; of the confirmation of idiots; of the confirmation of those who have not reached the use of reason when a protracted absence of the bishop is foreseen; of the confirmation of those stricken with pestilence which would endangers the bishop's life. Is the bishop bound to confirm in all these different cases? In the following consecutive treatment of these questions practical answers will be attempted.

It is commonly maintained that the bishop is not, or probably is not, obliged to confirm a dying person requesting confirmation.[157]

[157] Lehmkuhl, *Theologia Moralis* (2 vols., 12. ed., Friburgi Brisgoviae, 1914) Vol. II, n. 137; Bevilacqua, *De Episcopi Juribus ac Obligationibus* (Romae: Fredericus Pustet, 1921), n. 599; Prümmer, *Manuale Iuris Canonici*, p. 377; Ferreres, *Compendium Theologiae Moralis* (2 vols., 14

How is this absence of obligation explained? It is said, first of all, that this sacrament is not necessary for salvation; secondly, that it would be very difficult or morally impossible for the bishop to confirm all dying people who would ask for confirmation; thirdly, that since he could not confirm all such petitioners, he should not be considered obliged to confirm any, for if some were confirmed and others left unconfirmed there would be occasion for scandal. This is the usual manner in which any obligation on the bishop's part to confirm a dying person is explained away.[158] Regarding the absence of any law in the Code on giving confirmation to persons *in extremis* one author says: ". . . rightly so, because confirmation is not necessary for salvation, and a bishop cannot easily be obtained for such an occasion."[159]

An acquaintance with what some of the most distinguished theologians say on administering confirmation in danger of death does not incline one to the common opinion that a bishop has no obligation to confirm a dying person asking for confirmation; a knowledge of important particular legislation, which has been enacted on administering confirmation in danger of death, and to which the Holy See has given unqualified approval, makes one disposed to question the common opinion; and an understanding of the extremes to which the Holy See has gone to secure the administration of confirmation for infants and adults in danger of death compels one to deny that the bishop is absolutely exempt from all obligation to confirm a dying person requesting the sacrament. Regarding the lack of Code legislation on the point, an explanation will be suggested, or will suggest itself, later.

St. Thomas writes: "Therefore should confirmation be given

ed., Barcinone: Eugenius Subirana, 1928), II, n. 355; Genicot-Salsmans, *Institutiones Moralis Theologiae* (2 vols., 12. ed., Bruxelles; Dewit, 1931), Vol. II, n. 162; Augustine, *Commentary,* IV, 115; Aertyns-Damen, *Theoogia Moralis* (2 vols., 13. ed., Romae: Marietti, 1939), Vol. II, n. 88; Iorio, *Theologia Moralis* (3 vols., 6. ed., Neapoli: M. D'Auria, 1939), Vol. III, n. 96.

158 Cf. authors referred to in the preceding footnote.

159 Bevilacqua, *op. cit.,* n. 588.

to those about to die, in order that at the resurrection they may be perfect, according to the saying in Ephesians, IV, 13: 'Until we all come to the status of the perfect man, and to the measure of the age of the fulness of Christ', and therefore does Hugh of St. Victor say: 'It would be dangerous (*omino periculosum*) if one should happen to depart this life without confirmation, not that one should be condemned, unless perchance for contempt, but because he would suffer a privation of perfection'."[160] In the light of this teaching of St. Thomas, to which the Sacred Congregation for the Discipline of the Sacraments made special reference when legislating on the administration of confirmation,[161] it may indeed be questioned that the bishop has no obligation to administer confirmation to a dying person expressly desiring it. Seeing the grace which the sacrament confers, and the additional subsequent glory to which it entitles the dying person, how can the bishop be free from even a light obligation to confirm in view of the scandal that might arise from his failure to confirm *all* dying people? Is it not highly questionable that there will be any ground for scandal if the bishop, despite his reasonable effort to confirm the dying people who sent for him, should nevertheless fail to accommodate the wishes of all, and thus fall short in the ministration of confirmation to some of them?

Suarez says that as a rule and apart from incidental considerations people about to die are by all means (*omnino*) to be confirmed, because, as is evident, there is no reason why they should be deprived of such an augmentation and perfection of grace and glory.[162] Suarez apparently could not conceive of any justifiable practice whereby bishops universally abstained from giving confirmation to dying people to whom they could reasonably bring it, lest in failing to give it to others there might be occasion for scandal.

[160] *Summa Theologica,* Pars Tertia, Ques. LXXII, Art. VIII, ad 4.

[161] "Instructio pro simplici Sacerdote Sacramentum Confirmationis ex Sedis Apostolicae Delegatione administrante, die Feste Pentecostes. 1934"—*AAS,* XXVII (1935), 16.

[162] *Opera Omnia,* XX, Quaes. LXXII, Art. VIII, Sect. II, n. 6.

A plenary council for Latin America in 1902 made the following strong appeal to the bishops for whom it legislated: "We exhort all bishops that, as often as it can be done without prejudice to their pastoral duties, they should strive with all their energy (*totis viribus*) that infirm infants living in the episcopal city and not yet confirmed do not leave this world without the character of confirmation, in order that they may enjoy a greater glory in heaven by bearing the seal of such an august sacrament.[163] It need not be stressed that it is desirable that adults as well as infants should attain greater glory in heaven, and that therefore the bishop should by a death-bed administration of confirmation enable them also to secure additional glory. Certainly the decree of the aforementioned plenary council is couched in the most exacting terms short of legal obligation; and this decree was approved by the Sacred Congregation of the Council without any such proviso as: "Care being taken to avoid any scandal that might arise by exception of persons or places".

In an Instruction issued by the Sacred Congregation for the Discipline of the Sacraments, which has scarcely the restricted character of particular legislation, occur these words: "If there is question of a child so seriously ill that it may be said to be in danger of death, not only is it not forbidden to administer confirmation to him before the age of seven years, but it is expedient to do so, so that upon leaving this life he may, according to the doctrine of St. Thomas (III. q. 73, art. 8, ad 4) have greater glory in heaven."[164] Here it may be asked if confirmation should be administered to those in danger of death before attaining the use of reason, in order that they may secure a greater glory in heaven, should it not be administered *a fortiori* to adults,[165] for

[163] "Hortamur omnes episcopos ut quoties absque praejudicio aliorum munerum pastoralium fieri poterit, curent totis viribus ut infantes infirmi, degentes in civitate episcopali qui sacramentum confirmationis nondum receperunt, ex hac vita non discedant, absque charactere confirmationis, ut tanto sacramento insigniti majori in coelo gloria perfruantur."—*Acta et Decreta Concilii Plenarii Americae Latinae,* n. 519.

[164] *AAS,* XXVII (1935), 16.

[165] Cf. canon 745, § 1, 2°.

whom in addition to the obtaining of greater glory there is the utility of "being strengthened by the grace of this sacrament, so that in their last agony they may wrestle more successfully with the tempter"?[166] It is clear that the Instruction is referring directly to age when it speaks of the expediency of confirming certain infants under seven. However, the fact that the Instruction simply and expressly recommends the confirmation of these infants shows that the Holy See would rather see the minister trying to confirm as many of them as possible, than entertaining scruples that scandal might occur in case he failed to confirm all such infants.

The extreme pains which the Holy See will take to enable unconfirmed dying people to receive confirmation is revealed by a very extraordinary faculty which has been given to ordinaries in China. By apostolic indult these ordinaries can give all their priests the faculty of administering confirmation to both infants and adults in danger of death, even in the place of the bishop's residence, provided that no bishop is actually present and able to act.[167]

This is a very ususual faculty. When the Holy See gave authority for a few priests to give confirmation in South America, it said that it was compelled to do that; [168] in other words, it was only because of the extraordinary South American conditions that it could allow priests to administer confirmation there. Yet in China the ordinaries have an apostolic indult to delegate not one or a few, but all their priests to administer confirmation to infants and adults in danger of death. Evidently, if the Holy See did not

[166] "Conferences Romaines," *NRT,* XIII (1881), 189; cf. Marc-Gesterman-Raus, *Institutiones Morales Alphonsianae* (2 vols., 13. ed., Parisiis: Typis Emmanuelis Vitte, 1928), Vol. II, n. 1499.

[167] "Ordinarii loci ex Indulto Apostolicae Sedis delegare possunt omnibus suis sacerdotibus facultatem administrandi valide et licite sacram Confirmationem fidelibus sive adultis sive pueris in articulo mortis constitutis etiam in loco residentiae episcopi, absente tamen quocumque Episcopo vel gravi de causa impedito."—*Primum Concilium Sinense* (Zi-Ka-Wei: Typographia Missionis Catholicae, 1929), n. 273.

[168] Cf. *AAS,* XXVII (1935), 13.

consider the confirmation of all unconfirmed people in danger of death very important, it would not have given ordinaries in China such an exceptional and perhaps unprecedented faculty. In fact to the mind of the Holy See the confirmation of dying people is so important and its spiritual utility to such people is so tremendous that a pastor, bound to provide for the spiritual *advantage* as well as the spiritual necessity of his people, cannot generally consider himself exempt from the obligation to confirm death-bed petitioners, if he enjoys the necessary faculty to do so.

The opinion that bishops are not obliged to confirm *any* dying people, because of the alleged scandal that would accrue to their failure to confirm *all* such people, cannot be sustained in the light of the preceding paragraphs. In the arguments that have been presented the Holy See implicitly denies a general basis for this excuse.

That does not mean, however, that the bishop would be obliged to devote himself to this ministry with no regard for the proportionate hardship to himself, or with insufficient concern for the discharge of his other important episcopal duties. Cappello, who with some hesitation questions the opinion which exempts the bishop from any obligation in this matter, offers a suggestion which will help to determine when the bishop is under an obligation and when he is free from it. "It seems", he says, "that this teaching (which denies all obligation) ought not be admitted in the general form in which it is expressed. The particular circumstances should be considered and suitable distinctions made. If the person asking for confirmation in danger of death lives near the bishop's residence, so that the bishop can administer the sacrament to him without any inconvenience, who will say that the bishop is not bound even *sub levi* to confirm such a one?" [169] According to the opinion or teaching of Cappello, who, it will be noted, ignores the question of possible scandal due to apparent exception of persons, the bishop is bound at least *sub levi* to administer confirmation to a person requesting it in danger of death, when he can do so without an effort that is proportionately too

[169] *De Sacramentis,* I, n. 207.

great. The study pursued in the pages immediately preceding warrant a conclusion not less exacting that Cappello's. The bishop will sometimes be under an obligation.

Why, then, did the Code neglect to impose an obligation to confirm dying persons, at least when they ask to be confirmed? It cannot be because the Holy See regarded the confirmation of such people outside the sphere of pastoral duty.[170] The Legislator probably foresaw difficulties which made the imposition of a legal obligation seem inadvisable. If a legal obligation were imposed it would perhaps be impossible for some bishops to confirm all the dying people who would ask for it; and because of the unequal opportunities, or for some lack of opportunity, many dying people might be greatly perturbed.[171]Besides, if there were a legal obligation to give confirmation, the Holy See would surely be besieged by the bishops for faculties to delegate their priests to confirm,[172] yet consistently with the Holy See's policy of not permitting a very general delegation of priests, it would have to refuse the request of the bishops.[173] This, in turn, would seem to minimize the bishop's duty of confirming in danger of death. Then, too, the Holy See may have wished not to deny that *in some places* circumstances might exist which would excuse the bishop from confirming any dying person in danger of death.[174] Consequently the absence of a general legal obligation to confirm people in danger of death does not furnish a basis for the view that a moral obligation to perform this service is never present.

As subjects of confirmation idiots in general may be compared to sane people in danger of death. Regarding idiots, moralists say that confirmation may be fruitfully and lawfully administered to them.[175] If they have been without the use of reason from infancy, or if after lapsing into insanity they may be con-

[170] Cf. *supra,* footnotes nn. 167, 163.

[171] Cf. Lehmkuhl, *Theologia Moralis,* II, n. 137.

[172] Cf. *AAS,* XXVII (1935), 14.

[173] Cf. *AAS, loc. cit.*

[174] Cf. Lehmkuhl, *Theologia Moralis,* II, n. 137.

[175] Vermeersch, *Theologia Moralis,* III, n. 246; Noldin-Schmitt, *Summa Theologiae Moralis,* III, n. 91.

sidered disposed, there is no reason for deferring their confirmation.[176] Granted the lawfulness and fruitfulness of confirming them, it can be asked if there is an obligation to confirm them.

It has been seen that the Apostolic See considered the confirmation of infants in danger of death before attaining the use of reason expedient, so that they might have greater glory in heaven.[177] Idiots who have been such from infancy, or who are in the state of grace after lapsing into insanity, are, in so far as they are capable of receiving a title to greater glory,[178] in the same condition as infants. Therefore their confirmation would be at least "expedient". But it has been seen that it is not a mere matter of expediency, but also one of obligation for a pastor of souls to secure for his people, whatever they be, that right to the greater glory which the sacrament of confirmation gives them.[179] Therefore a bishop is bound to administer confirmation to the idiots under his pastoral care that they may obtain greater glory in heaven. It would in general be too hazardous to wait to see if they will acquire or recover the use of reason.[180]

If there is not a grave obligation to confirm an individual sane person who asks for confirmation,[181] then it would be hard to prove that there would be a grave obligation to confirm an individual insane person. It seems that a bishop would be excused from any obligation, if there were very much difficulty in administering confirmation to an insane person.[182] In particular cases the confirmation of these people might be an occasion for hatred of or opposition to the Church. This could easily happen when insane people are congregated in a public mental institu-

[176] Suarez, *Opera Omnia*, Vol. XX, Quaes. LXXII, Art. VIII, Sec. II, n. 5.

[177] Cf. *Supra*, footnote 163.

[178] Cf. Cappello, *De Sacramentis*, I, n. 81.

[179] Cf. Vermeersch, *Theologia Moralis*, III, n. 181.

[180] Cf. Suarez, *Opera Omnia*, Vol. XX, Quaes, LXXII, Art. VIII, Sec. II, n. 5.

[181] Cf. Cappello, *De Sacramentis*, I, n. 207.

[182] Cf. Cappello, *loc. cit.*

tion, in which any known religious interference with the inmates would arouse a general protest. In such circumstances Vermeersch's advice would be applicable, namely, that one may, or should, abstain from administering the sacraments even to one in extreme necessity, for instance, to an infant going to die without baptism, in order to avoid stirring up hatred for the Church.[183]

If the bishop is visiting or confirming in a part of an extensive diocese, and it is foreseen that he will not be able to go there for about five years more, it is apropos to ask is he obliged to confirm those children who are now under seven years but who at the next visitation will be from one to five years past seven? It is *permissible* to confirm infants who have not reached the use of reason, when a long absence of the bishop is anticipated. This is expressly stated in the Instruction of 1934.[184] A commentary on this point which appears in *Il Monitore Ecclesiastico* goes so far as to say that in very large dioceses, particularly in mountainous regions where the bishop can repeat the visitation only every four or five years, it is evident (*e chiaro*) that he may lawfully admit to confirmation children of six, five or four years; yes, even of three or two.[185] The reason for this is that otherwise these children after reaching the use of reason would have to remain too long exposed to the attacks of Satan, without the protection which confirmation is designed to give.[186] But, if it is lawful to confirm children before they have reached the age of seven in order to ensure that the appropriate spiritual armour will not be long wanting to them after the beginning of life's combat with evil, then it seems *even a pastoral duty* to anticipate the ministration of confirmation before they have attained the age of reason, when that is the only way of meeting their spiritual needs which would otherwise remain unattended over an appreciable span of time. When the bishop foresees a prolonged absence, there seems to be an obligation on his part to confirm the children who are

[183] *Theologia Moralis*, III, n. 197.
[184] *AAS*, XXVII (1935), 16; cf. canon 788.
[185] V (1935), III.
[186] *Loc. cit.*

now under seven, but who at the time of the next episcopal visitation will be much over seven.

It is commonly held that a pastor is bound to administer only the necessary sacraments during an epidemic which would endanger his life.[187] Since confirmation is in no circumstances considered one of the necessary sacraments,[188] it follows that the bishop is not obliged to administer it with danger to his life during a time of epidemic. Benedict XIV says that the practice of St. Charles Borromeo in administering Confirmation to people of Milan during the dreadful plague (1576) was a heroic example from which no obligation can be deduced.[189]

But though there is no obligation on the bishop to administer confirmation with danger to his life during an epidemic, it would be fitting if he did so, even at so serious a risk. The reason is that as a pastor of souls he should set his people and priests an example of the highest virtue.[190] Such heroic devotion to duty would be most edifying to all his subjects.[191]

Article 6. Obligation of Ordinary Impeded from Confirming or Lacking the Power to Confirm

Canon 785, § 3: *Ordinarius legitima causa impeditus aut potestate confirmandi carens, debet, quoad fieri possit, saltem intra quinquennium providere ut suis subditis hoc sacramentum administretur.*

The Holy See is so eager to see the faithful of all parts of the diocese given an opportunity at least every five years for receiving confirmation that it requires provision to be made for this whenever the ordinary is impeded from confirming or lacks the power to do so. The obligation to call a minister rests on two people in the circumstances envisioned in paragraph 3 of the canon. It

[187] Lehmkuhl, *Theologia Moralis,* II, n. 51; Vermeersch, *Theologia Moralis,* III, n. 197; Merkelback, *Summa,* III, n. 2303.

[188] Benedict XIV, *De Synodo Dioecesana,* Lib. VII, cap. 10, n. 9.

[189] *De Synodo Dioecesana,* Lib. XIII, cap. 19, nn. 5 ff.; cf. "Conferences Romaines," *Revue Theologique,* XIII (1881), 181 ff.

[190] Cf. Cappello, *De Sacramentis,* I, n. 20.

[191] Cf. Benedict XIV, *De Synodo Dioecesana,* Lib. XIII, cap. 19, n. 12.

applies first of all to the bishop of a diocese who is *legitimately* impeded from confirming. Legitimate causes preventing the bishop from administering confirmation in his entire diocese every five years would be the causes contemplated in canon 439, § 1. So also would be protracted illness or advanced age.[192] Secondly the obligation to obtain a bishop for confirmation rests on an ordinary who does not possess the power of confirming. This would refer to a vicar capitular (administrator), or to a priest,[193] on whom the government of the diocese has devolved in the circumstances mentioned in canon 439, § 1.

If no bishop were invited in to administer confirmation, while the diocese was vacant or its bishop impeded,[194] the whole diocese, or at least a part of it, might have no opportunity of confirmation for six or seven years. That is why the vicar capitular (administrator), or the other priest who administers the diocese temporarily, is obliged to see that no part of the diocese is denied confirmation for more than five years.[195]

It is understood that in the circumstances in which the ordinary is prevented from confirming personally, it will sometimes be very difficult, if not impossible, to procure another minister for confirmation.[196] In a time of persecution, for example, there might be no possibility of finding any bishop to confirm. Therefore does the canon say "in so far as it is possible" arrangements would be made to have confirmation administered every five years. Unless it is unavoidable, a lapse of more than five years cannot be tolerated.

Article 7. Observance of Quinquennial Administration of Confirmation Urged by Legal Sanction

Canon 785, § 4: *Si graviter neglexerit* (*Ordinarius*) *sacramentum confirmationis suis subditis per se vel per alium ministrare, servetur praescriptum can.* 274, *n.* 4.

[192] Cf. Augustine, *Commentary*, IV, III.
[193] Cf. Vermeersch-Creusen, *Epitome*, I, n. 317.
[194] Canon 429 § 1.
[195] Cf. *Decr. Auth. S.R.C., Sanctae Luciae,* 14 apr. 1877, n. 3416.
[196] Cf. Blat, *Commentarium,* vol. III, Pars I, n. 79.

Because of the connection of paragraph 4 with the preceding paragraphs of canon 785 the subject of the verb *neglexerit* must of necessity be assumed to be the word *Ordinarius*.[197] If, then, any ordinary[198] is guilty of grave negligence, because he neither confirms personally nor has another do it for him for over five years, the matter may be reported to the Roman Pontiff by the Archbishop. Canon 274, 4°, which is to take effect when the ordinary is seriously remiss in his duty regarding the administration of confirmation, says that his metropolitan should inform the Holy Father about abuses regarding ecclesiastical discipline in the suffragan see.

It is only when the metropolitan prudently judges that there has been objectively a grave abuse on the part of his suffragan ordinary that he may send a complaint to the Holy See.[199] Consequently, if a bishop who was impeded from confirming, or if another ordinary who lacked the power to confirm, were unable to have confirmation administered, there would be no justification for informing the Supreme Pontiff. The Holy See has indeed indicated its grave concern to see all the people given adequate facility for receiving confirmation, but it is only grave negligence in furnishing the people with sufficient opportunity for confirmation that the Legislator aims to prevent when he subjects its administration to the surveilance of the metropolitan.

Article 8. Offerings to Minister

The *Taxa Innocentiana,* which became general law October 8, 1676, forbade ministers to accept any offerings on the occasion of administering the sacraments,[200] and reprobated every contrary custom as simoniacal.[201] Subsequently there were many severe prohibitions against accepting any offerings for administering confirmation.[202] Particular responses show how adverse the Holy

[197] Cf. Blat, *Commentarium,* Vol. III, Pars I, n. 79.

[198] Cf. canon 198; Vermeersch-Creusen, *Epitome,* I, n. 317.

[199] Cf. Blat, *Commentarium,* Vol. III, Pars I, n. 79.

[200] Pallottini, s.v. "Taxa," n. 32.

[201] Cf. Ferreris, *Bibliotheca,* s.v. "Confirmatio," nn. 27, 28.

[202] Cf. Ferreris, *loc. cit.,* nn. 24-29; Lucidi, *De Visitatione Sacrorum Liminum* (2 vols., 3. ed., Romae, 1883), Vol. I, nn. 58-59.

See has been to the acceptance of offerings for even the incidental expenses which the bishop had in administering confirmation.[203]

After the publication of the Code there are some who maintain that the bishop may not accept any offerings on the occasion of administering confirmation, and that he must also bear the expenses that he incurs when he has to travel to administer it.[204] But this opinion can hardly be sustained. It is not supported by the Code.

The Code says: "Regardless of the reason or the occasion, the minister shall not either directly or indirectly exact or ask for any remuneration in administering the sacraments, besides the offerings referred to in canon 1507.[205] Canon 1507 says in part that it pertains to the provincial council or a convention of the bishops of the province to determine the offerings to be made on the occasion of the administration of the sacraments. It may be noted, however, that should the matter not have been determined by the provincial council or by the assembled bishops of the province, then it is admissible to follow any legitimate custom that may exist.[206]

Under the Code then, the minister of the sacraments has a right to ask for what has been determined in accordance with canon 1507, or by legitimate custom. Consequently, if either the ruling referred to in canon 1507 or a proper custom permits the bishop to ask for an offering when he administers confirmation, then he has a right to receive it.

If a law or a decree of the bishops gives the minister of confirmation a right to a honorarium the matter is settled. On the

[203] Cf. *Anceletica Juris Pontificii,* X (1869), 628.

[204] Marc-Gesterman-Raus, *Institutiones Morales Alphonsianae* (2 vols., 18. ed., Lugduni: Typis Emanuelis Vitte, 1927), II, n. 1498; Villien, *History and Liturgy of the Sacraments,* English Translation by Edwards (London: Burns Oates, 1932), p. 84.

[205] Canon 736.

[206] Cf. canon 463, § 1; Claeys-Bouuaert-Simenon, *Manuale Juris Canonici* (3 vols., Gandae et Leodii, 1934), Vol. III (4. ed., 1934), n. 259; Vermeersch-Creusen, *Epitome,* II, n. 827; Cappello, *De Sacramentis,* I, n. 96.

other hand, it is sometimes difficult to determine whether or not custom gives the bishop a right to ask for an offering for administering confirmation. It would have to be ascertained if there was a custom vested with all the qualities necessary to give it the force of law.[207]

But whatever one may hold regarding the existence or the non-existence of a title to an offering for administering confirmation, it is admitted that the bishop may ask that his incidental expenses be taken care of when he goes around his diocese for the purpose of administering confirmation.[208] Nor is he forbidden under Code law to receive offerings voluntarily made. The common law says that he may not *demand* or *ask for* more than has been stipulated by the proper authority.[209] If he is making the diocesan visitation at the time he is administering confirmation, he is forbidden indeed to accept any offerings or gifts by reason of the visitation, but not for other reasons.

This has been only an attempt to show what the bishop may accept or demand without contravening the law or legitimate custom. The expediency of a practice in this matter is to be determined in the light of the considerations proposed to bishops by the Council of Trent.[210]

[207] Cf. canons 25-30.

[208] Cappello, *De Sacramentis,* I, n. 74.

[209] Cf. Woywod, *A Practical Commentary on the Code of Canon Law* (2 vols., 4. ed., New York: Joseph Wagner, 1932), I, 327.

[210] Sess. XXV, *de ref.,* c. 1.

CHAPTER IV

THE EXTRAORDINARY MINISTER OF CONFIRMATION

ARTICLE 1.—REVIEW OF THE PRIEST-MINISTER'S ACTIVITY UP TO THE CODE

In the previous brief historical study on the priest-minister of confirmation the times, places, and other circumstances in which he exercised his extraordinary function have been summarily examined.[1] In the fourth century priests at Alexandria and throughout Egypt confirmed in the absence of a bishop.[2] In the fifth and sixth centuries Spanish and Gallican priests probably enjoyed the faculty of confirming in certain contingencies.[3] By express authorization which the Pope gave in view of the unusual circumstances, priests confirmed in Sicily during the seventh century.[4] In the meantime, that is, since the fourth century, the practice first noted as peculiar to Egypt[5] must have been extending itself in the East,[6] for by the time of the Photian revolt is was widely established there.[7] In the thirteenth, fourteenth and fifteenth centuries priests of the Franciscan Order engaged in pioneer work were given the faculty of confirming.[8] Since then priests in missionary countries have time and again been given the faculty to confirm.[9]

In view of the important part which the priest has had as a minister of confirmation, it seems surprising that some of the

[1] Cf. Chap. I, Art. 2.

[2] Cf. St. Ambrosius, *Commentaria in Epist. ad Ephesios—MPG*, XVII, 388; (Anonymous), *Quaes. in Nov. et Vet. Test.—MPG,* XXV, 232.

[3] Cf. Chap. I, Art. 2.

[4] Cf. Gregory I, *Ep. XXVI—MPL,* LXXVII, 696.

[5] Cf. *Supra,* footnote 2.

[6] Cf. *Echos D'Orient,* XXIX (1930), 8.

[7] Cf. *Jus Pontificium,* II (1931), 137.

[8] Cf. *De Synodo Dioecesana,* Lib. VII, cap. 7, n. 6.

[9] Cf. Fontes, nn. 279, 305, 357, 432, 368, 485.

Scholastics denied his potentiality to be a minister of confirmation;[10] and that the Council of Trent, after discussing the point,[11] hesitated to make any statement on the priest-minister. It was only in the capacity of theologian or canonist that Pope Benedict XIV gave his lucid exposition of the doctrine on the extraordinary minister of confirmation.[12]

It might indeed be asked why there existed contradictory teaching for so long, and why the councils, when given an opportunity, did not give a decisive statement? It seems that an explanation can be found. In the *Decretum* of Gratian there is a canon on the minister of confirmation which has as its alleged source a decretal letter of Pope Eusebius (309-310). This canon reads: "The sacrament of imposition of hands is to be regarded with great veneration. This imposition cannot be performed by anyone except the *high priests.* Nor do we read or know that in the times of the Apostles is was performed by others than by the Apostles themselves. It never can, and it never must, be done by others than those who take their place. For in any presumption to the contrary, the sacrament must be regarded null and void, and will never be considered one of the Sacraments of the Church." [13] This spurious [14] canon seems to rule out the possibility of a priest's ever being able to act as the minister of confirmation. Its ruling is so absolute than one could hardly dare to presume that a priest could perhaps be given a faculty or delegation to administer confirmation. Indeed, in as far as this supposititious document was

[10] Cf. Chap. I, footnote 51.

[11] Cf. Pallavicino, *Historia Concilii Tridentini,* Lib. VII, cap. 7.

[12] *De Synodo Dioecesana,* Lib. VII, cap. VII, VIII, X.

[13] "Manus quoque impositionis sacramentum magna veneratione tenendum est, quod ab aliis perfici non potest, nisi a summis sacerdotibus, necque tempore apostolorum ab aliis, quam ab ipsis apostolis legitur aut scitur peractum esse, nec ab aliis quam ab his qui eorum tenent locum unquam perfici potest aut fieri debet. Nam si aliter praesumptum fuerit, irritum habeatur et vacuum et inter Ecclesiastica numquam reputabitur sacramenta."—C.4, D.V, *de cons.*

[14] Van Espen, *Jus Ecclesiasticum Universum,* Tom. I, Pars II, Tit. III, *De Sacramento Confirmationis,* n. 1.

not unknown to the writers and inasmuch as its papal origin was not questioned by them, it seems logical and necessary to deny that a priest could be delegated to confirm. Besides, such a conclusion would seem to have been supported by two other canons, which had their indisputable source in the decretals of Innocent I and Gelasius I.[15] There was of course the precedent which Gregory I had set by authorizing priests to confirm.[16] To modern times that would have almost the force of an *ab esse ad posse* argument; but it was not accepted as such by some of the Scholastics.[17] Hadrian VI (1522-1523) had maintained before his elevation to the papacy that the concession Gregory had given to the priests of Cagliari was not the faculty to confirm, but a permission to perform a mere ceremonial rite,[18] though, after becoming Pope, Hadrian himself is known to have given priests authority to confirm.[19]

Apparently Eugene IV (1431-1447)[20] did not consider it expedient to be more explicit than he was regarding the priest and confirmation.

The Council of Trent (1545-1563) must have thought that it was sufficient to condemn the reformers' errors on confirmation[21] without settling what was still a moot point even among Catholics. Moreover, though a statement on the priest-minister seemed more or less called for at the Council of Trent,[22] it might only have confirmed heretics in their errors if the Council had asserted that the priest could in any circumstances administer confirmation.[23]

[15] C. 119, D. IV, *de cons;* c. 2, D. XCV.
[16] *Ep. XXVI—MPL,* LXXVII, 695.
[17] Cf. Chap. I, footnote 51.
[18] Cf. Chardon, *Histoire des Sacraments,* II, 501.
[19] Cf. Benedict XIV, *De Synodo Dioecesana,* Lib. VII, cap. 7, n. 6.
[20] Cf. Denzinger, *Enchiridion,* n. 697.
[21] Cf. O'Dwyre, *Confirmation,* p. 165.
[22] Cf. Pallavicino, *Historia Concilii Tridentini,* Lib. VII, cap. 7.
[23] Cf. Pallottini, XVI, s.v. "Sacramentum Confirmationis," nn. 22-23.

Article 2.—The Code's Characterization of Extraordinary Minister

Canon 782, § 2: *Extraordinarius minister [confirmationis] est presbyter, cui vel iure communi vel peculiari Sedis Apostolicae indulto ea facultas concessa sit.*

At the present time a Saintebeuve [24] could no longer question the possibility of a priest's being delegated to confirm. The Code asserts that a priest by common law or apostolic indult is a minister, the extraordinary minister, of confirmation.

From what has been learned about the extraordinary minister in the historical section one can readily appreciate and put together the elements of a definition of extraordinary minister as found in Blat.[25] It might run: "The extraordinary minister of confirmation is a priest who by the divine law does not derive the power to be a minister from the order he has received, but who by the plentitude of power of the Roman Pontiff is delegated to administer confirmation in exceptional circumstances." The person to whom the delegation of the Apostolic See is given must be a priest. A deacon could not be delegated to administer confirmation, because the administration of confirmation demands essentially an exercise of the sacerdotal order.[26] 2Just as the Pope cannot give a cleric in minor orders the faculty to absolve from sin, so also he cannot give a deacon or any other one except a priest the power to confirm.[27]

A priest's delegation is now for the first time established by the common law. Strictly considered, the Code attaches the faculty to certain ecclesiastical offices,[28] and the priest who succeeds to one of these offices receives *eo ipso* a limited faculty of confirming. In this way a priest who becomes an abbot or prelate *nullius* is

[24] Cf. *Tractatus de Sacramento Confirmationis*, p. 450.

[25] *Commentarium*, Vol. III, Pars I, n. 76.

[26] Cf. Wernz-Vidal, *Ius Canonicum*, Vol. IV, Pars I, n. 55.

[27] Cf. Clarke, "The Minister of the Sacrament of Confirmation," *Australasian Catholic Record*, I (1924), 18.

[28] Cf. Canons 319, 308.

invested with the power to administer confirmation. The expediency and convenience of this provision of law is evident to anyone who considers the nature and eminence [29] of the offices which include in themselves the power to confirm.[30]

The old, customary method of delegating priests to confirm is still retained. The reason is that there will be many cases which require the delegation of a priest for confirmation but which, in view of the Holy See's characteristic reluctance to give the faculty to priests, can hardly be provided for by the common law.[31] This holds particularly while the Holy See is not disposed to leave the final judgment on the necessity and advisability of delegating the priest to the discretion of a local ordinary.[32]

Modern instances of delegation by Apostolic Indult can be found in China, and Latin America.[33]

Whether this delegation of a priest to confirm is necessarily reserved to the Pope has been, and still is, a disputed point.[34] As a practical rule, it is certain that without delegation from the Holy Father no priest can now validly administer the sacrament of confirmation.[35] Delegation received from a bishop would not suffice.

It has been already noted that Apostolic delegation need not come directly from the Pope, but with papal authority it may be granted by a Roman Congregation,[36] by an Apostolic Delegate [37] or by a local ordinary.[38]

[29] Cf. *AAS,* XXVII (1935), 12, *in fine.*

[30] Cf. canons 239, 294, 323.

[31] Cf. Benedictus XIV, Inst. *Eo quamvis tempore,* 4 maii 1745, § 8—*Fontes,* n. 357.

[32] *Loc. cit.*

[33] Cf. *AAS,* XXXI (1939), 224; *Primum Concilium Sinense,* n. 273.

[34] Cf. Cappello, *De Sacramentis,* I, n. 205.

[35] Cf. Benedict XIV, *De Synodo Dioecesana,* Lib. VII, cap. 8, n. 7.

[36] Cf. AAS, XXXI (1939), 224.

[37] Cf. *Periodica,* XII (1923), (131).

[38] Cf. *Primum Concilium Sinense,* n. 273.

Article 3.—What the Priest Receives in His Faculty To Confirm

The most difficult problem with regard to confirmation is perhaps to determine what precisely a priest receives by the apostolic delegation which enables him to administer this sacrament. Is it a power of orders? Is is jurisdiction? Or is it something distinct from orders and jurisdiction? It appears that an acceptable solution can be gleaned from the writings of the various theologians and canonists who have grappled with the question.

There have been some who held that the priest could confirm in virtue of his priesthood without any delegation from a higher authority.[39] In other words, he does not receive anything by delegation on which the validity of his act of confirming is conditioned. In support of this opinion reasons are offered which are admittedly very difficult to refute.[40]

What the priest receives by delegation cannot be jurisdiction.[41] Jurisdiction is not at all necessary for the valid administration of confirmation. A bishop retains the power of confirming after he has been deprived of all his jurisdiction.[42] Besides, it does not pertain to the nature of confirmation to require jurisdictional power in its minister, as is required in the dispenser of the sacrament of penance.[43]

Neither can the priest receive by delegation a power of orders; for it cannot be that the Pope *by an act of jurisdiction* delegates to the priest a power of orders.[44] It seems inconceivable that a power of orders could be transmitted by letter or telephone to a

[39] Fortescue, *The Orthodox Eastern Church,* p. 421; Dölger *apud* Lehmkuhl, *Theologia Moralis,* II, n. 133.

[40] Cf. Clarke, "The Minister of the Sacrament of Confirmation," *ACR,* I (1924), 17.

[41] Lehmkuhl, *Theologia Moralis,* II, n. 134; Vermeersch-Creusen, *Epitome,* II, n. 61; Diekamp. *Theologiae Dogmaticae Manuale* (2 vols., 6 ed., Parisiis: Declee et Socii, 1934), II, 126; Ballerini-Palmieri, *Opus Theologicum Morale* (7 vols., Prati, 1889-1893), IV, n. 16; Clarke, *ACR,* I, 19.

[42] Cf. p. 85.

[43] Lehmkuhl, *op. cit.,* Vol. II, n. 135.

[44] Cf. Clarke, *ACR,* I, 17.

priest hundreds of miles away.[45] But, though the priest does not receive a power of orders by apostolic delegation, it is agreed that he confirms by virtue of a power of orders.[46] Therefore it seems necessary to conclude that by reason of his priesthood and independently of apostolic delegation he is capable of administering the sacrament of confirmation.[47] Logical as that explanation may seem, it is not without grave difficulties. If a priest confirm by virtue of his priesthood, then it seems necessary to hold that like a bishop he cannot be prevented from the valid exercise of this faculty; and that confirmation administered by him will always be valid, just as it is valid in the case of its administration by any bishop whatever.[48] Where jurisdiction is not required, how can the Church render ineffectual an exercise of the power of orders? It does not seem that she can.[49] And yet she does not recognize the validity of confirmation, when it is administered by priests lacking pontifical delegation.

Nicholas I (858-867) would not admit the validity of confirmation administered to the Bulgarians by priests who did not possess pontifical delegation.[50] Innocent III (1198-1216) took the same attitude to confirmation administered by Latin priests in Constantinople, because they had not conceived authorization from Rome. Innocent IV (1243-1254) acted similarly.[51] Clement VII (1523-1534) implied that confirmation could not be validly administered by any priest who did not possess delegation from the Roman Pontiff.[52] Finally, in our own time Pius X has implicitly condemned the opinion that the priest can confirm by reason of

[45] Cf. Connell, "The Episcopate," *ER*, LXXII (1925), 342.

[46] Cf. Wernz-Vidal, *Ius Canonicum*, Vol. IV, Pars I, n. 55; Bellarmine, *Opera Omnia*, III, 232.

[47] Cf. Clarke, *ACR*, I (1924), 17.

[48] Cf. O'Dwyre, *Confirmation*, p. 171.

[49] Cf. O'Dwyre, *loc. cit.*

[50] *Ep. ad Arduicum Archiepiscopum Vestontionensem*—*MPL*, CXIX, 921.

[51] Ep. "*Sub catholicae,*" 6 mart. 1254, § 3, n. 4—*Fontes*, n. 34.

[52] Ep. "*Super quibusdam*" ad Consolatorem, Catholicon Armenorum, 29 sept. 1351—*Fontes*, n. 42; Cf. also Denzinger, *Enchiridion*, nn. 573-574.

his priesthood alone.[53] Therefore, because of the many instrinsic difficulties, if not *a fortiori* by reason of the authoritative condemnations, the opinion seems altogether untenable that the priest receives nothing essential for confirmation by apostolic delegation.

But, it appears that this essential thing which is conferred on a priest by delegation is neither jurisdiction nor a power of orders. It is, however, something which belongs to the bishop by reason of his episcopate.[54] Nor can it be due immediately to the episcopal order, for otherwise a priest as such would never be able to confirm.

An explanation of this "something" will be admissible it seems, in proportion to the account which is taken of the nature of the sacrament of confirmation.[55] Just as one argues the necessity of jurisdiction from the concept of the judicial nature of penance, so from an understanding of the nature of confirmation it is logical to deduce that it demands a certain quality in the minister.

"Confirmation" according to Suarez, "is a sacrament instituted primarily to give men the fullness of the Holy Ghost, and the more abundant helps by which they are strengthened to profess and practice their faith: it is administered to give them the character by which they are constituted soldiers of Christ." [56] That it is the purpose of confirmation to render men strong and courageous in the profession of their faith, that it is to make them soldiers of Christ, is the common teaching of theologians.[57] In other words, by confirmation a person is constituted a soldier in the spiritual order, just as by the process of military enrollment a

[53] Ep. *"Ex quo,"* 26 dec. 1910: " . . . cui [i.e., doctrinae quae asserit Ecclesiae competere ius circa ipsam sacramentorum substantiam aliquam facere innovationem] haud minus absonum est, validam habendam esse Confirmationem a quovis presbytero collatam."—AAS, III (1911), 119; Cappello, *De Sacramentis,* I, n. 204.

[54] Cf. p.

[55] Lehmkuhl, *Theologia Moralis,* II, n. 136.

[56] *Opera Omnia,* XX, Quaest. LXIII, Art. IV, Sec. I, n. 7.

[57] Cf. Vermeersch, *Theologia Moralis,* III, 203; Noldin-Schmitt, *Summa,* III, n. 84; Cappello, *De Sacramentis,* I, n. 193; Lehmkuhl, *Theologia Moralis,* II, n. 135.

man becomes a soldier in the natural order.[58] Now, in civil society it belongs properly to the chief, the general, the king, to admit men to the status of soldiers. The officers of lower rank can receive men into the army only with delegated authority. But there is an anology between the natural and the supernatural life, between civil and ecclesiastical society.

Accordingly it rightly pertains to the bishop as the fitting ecclesiastical chieftain, not by reason of his jurisdiction,[59] nor by reason of his episcopal order [60] but by reason of his ecclesiastical dignity to constitute soldiers of the spiritual order. This power cannot belong to the bishop by reason of his episcopate, for otherwise, as already noted, nobody but a bishop could ever confirm; nor does it belong to him because of jurisdiction, for even after all his jurisdiction is taken away he still retains the faculty to confirm. It belongs to him, therefore, it would seem, on account of the preeminence which the episcopate gives him, by reason of a *prelatio*,[61] which results from the episcopate but which is not necessarily dependent on it.

To continue the analogy, it is fitting that an inferior officer in a religious society, like his counterpart in civil society, should be capable of being commissioned to enroll soldiers of Christ.[62] That is actually what is done when a priest is delegated to confirm.

It appears, then, that what the priest receives is a revocable grant of that dignity [63] or of that preeminence by reason of which the bishop is able to constitute soldiers of Christ. That is not to say that it is strictly in virtue of the borrowed preeminence that

[58] Cf. Lehmkuhl, *Theologia Moralis,* II, n. 135.

[59] Cf. *supra,* p. 162.

[60] Cf. *supra,* p. 165.

[61] Cf. Clarke, "The Minister of the Sacrament of Confirmation," *ACR,* I (1924), 18.

[62] Lehmkukhl, *Theologia Moralis,* II, n. 135.

[63] Authors use different terms to designate the quality given a priest, but they are all synonymous. Clarke has "Prelatio," *ACR,* I, 19; Van Noort, "Dignitas Excellens," *op. cit.*

a priest confirms. Rather this is considered as a condition;[64] and given this condition a priest confirms by an exercise of his priestly order.[65]

At the present time this appears to be the most common explanation of the quality that is communicated to a priest in order to enable him to administer confirmation. In its favor it can be said that it has regard for the nature and purpose of the sacrament of confirmation. Then too, it commends itself rather generally because it avoids the difficulties with which any theory of orders or jurisdiction is necessarily fraught. Though no writer perhaps is bold enough to say that it is the final solution of a grave problem of long standing, it does seem that it must be accepted as the most satisfactory exposition that is yet available.

Article 4.—Canon 209 and Delegation for Confirming

Though the priest does not receive jurisdiction in his faculty to confirm, it is pertinent to enquire if any principle which governs the supplying of jurisdiction is applicable in connection with the faculty of confirming. In particular, it should be asked whether the principle of canon 209 can be applied with reference to this faculty. One of the findings of Miaskiewicz is that canon 209 is not limited to the strictly jurisdictional sphere of action.[66] He shows that in circumstances paralled to those envisioned by canon 209 the Church will supply the quality necessary for valid assistance at marriage and *sponsalia*.[76] He makes no reference to the faculty of confirming, apparently because it would have been impossible to apply canon 209 to that faculty. If the ultimate reason for the Church's supplying of jurisdiction and of similar necessary qualities is because the common good and social utility

[64] Cf. McDonald, "The Sacrament of Extreme Unction," *ITQ*, II (1907), 338.

[65] Cappello, *De Sacramentis*, I, n. 204; Wernz-Vidal, *Ius Canonicum*, Vol. IV, Pars I, n. 55.

[66] *Supplied Jurisdiction According to Canon* 209, The Catholic University of America, Canon Law Studies, n. 122 (Washington, D. C.: The Catholic University of America, 1939), p. 312, n. 13.

[67] *Op. cit.*, 256, 281.

are in jeopardy,[68] then it can hardly be supposed that the Church would supply in the case of the faculty of confirming.[69] There is scarcely any parallel between the administration of confirmation and the instances in which Miaskiewicz[70] finds the Church supplying her needed jurisdiction.[71] Furthermore, owing to the caution which the Church employs in giving the faculty of confirming, it would be difficult to conceive that in the act of confirming there would be present the necessary basis whereon the Church supplies her powers in the light of canon 209; and since the administration of confirmation is not in the sphere of the internal forum, the applicability of canon 207, § 2, is not to be considered.

Regarding an ordinary using his delegated authority to commission priests to confirm, it might appear that there may be occasion for the application of canon 209. In this instance the ordinary is exercising jurisdiction, and a real doubt might arise as to the scope of his faculty: for instance, concerning the number of priests he has pontifical authority to delegate.

Regarding some of the conditions that are attached to the ordinary's faculty of delegating in missionary countries, Vermeersch says that these conditions regard the lawful but not the valid use of the faculty.[72] Vromant is in agreement with Vermeersch.[73] Therefore it seems to follow that when an ordinary delegates (subdelegates) priests to confirm, the circumstances necessary for the application of canon 209 will not ever be present.

Article 5.—Exceptional Conditions in Which Priests are Delegated

In the historical section it has been seen that the Holy See has been accustomed to delegate a priest to confirm only in exceptional,

[68] Cf. Miaskiewicz, *op. cit.*, p. 235.
[69] Cf. *Il Monitore Ecclesiastico*, 4 series, I (1919), 81.
[70] *Op. cit.*, p. 271 ff.
[71] *Il Monitore Ecclesiastico*, 4 series, IX (1927), 55.
[72] *Periodica*, XI (1922), (114).
[73] *Commentarium in Formulam Tertiam*, p. 29.

pressing circumstances.[74] After the Code the same reluctance on the part of the Holy See to delegate a priest for confirmation is still in evidence. In fact, the Instruction issued by the Sacred Congregation for the Discipline of the Sacraments in 1934 would seem to indicate that the faculty is obtained now only with greater difficulty than before. It states that the faculty is given to priests in the very extraordinary conditions that exist in certain regions of Latin America, and that in these places it is only for a grave and urgent reason and under moral compulsion (*quodammodo compellatur*) that the Holy See gives priests delegation to confirm.[75]

Zerba, commenting on the Instruction, writes that the dioceses to which these faculties were given are more extensive territorially than the whole of France or Italy. "Besides," he goes on to say, "they are without means of transportation; they have a severe climate, rugged mountains and large impassable rivers; they contain countless inhabitants widely scattered in the large cities, in villages far from the bishop's residence, in the open country and in the forests; such are the general conditions, in fact, that during his term of office the bishop cannot make a complete diocesan visitation."[76] As for population, when the bishop of Concepcion, Chile, applied to Pope Leo XIII for faculties for some of his priests, he reported that he had a million people in his diocese.[77]

Truly, then, the conditions in which priests are delegated in parts of Latin America are very unusual, and in the circumstances there was a crying need for the delegation of priests to confirm. But it appears that it was only in these conditions, which can scarcely be duplicated elsewhere, that the faculty of confirming could have been conceded.[78]

Some European bishops asked if the faculty which Latin American ordinaries had, namely, to delegate priests, could be

[74] Cf. Chap. I, Art. 2.

[75] "Instructio pro Simplice Sacerdote . . . " *AAS*, XXVII (1935), 13.

[76] *Apollinaris*, VIII (1935), 43.

[77] S.C.S. Off., 4 mart. 1903—*Collectanea*, n. 2161.

[78] *Perfice Munus*, X (1935), 82.

extended to Europe, when similar conditions existed. To this request the Sacred Congregation gave a negative answer; and said that it was the mind of the Holy See that there should be no change in the discipline which had hitherto been observed, and to which no exception had been allowed save for a few cases in South America, where owing to extraordinary circumstances the common law could not be observed.[79] Any other ordinaries who might be thinking of asking for the faculty of delegating some of their priests to confirm were advised to ask the Holy See for an auxiliary or coadjutor, or to obtain the aid of a neighboring bishop for the administration of confirmation.[80] This resolution of the Congregation is reproduced in the Instruction of 1934 as a general norm to be followed indefinitely.

Zerba relates that during the influenza epidemic of a few years ago, when many children were dying without confirmation, a large Italian Archdiocese petitioned Rome for the delegation of priests for confirmation, but the petition was denied.[81] Likewise an anonymous commentator in the *Periodica*[82] remarks that in the Namur and other cases mentioned in the Instruction of 1934 it was specifically delegation to confirm children seriously ill that was requested for priests, and yet the Holy See did not deem it opportune to accede to the request.

All this goes to show that generally it is extremely difficult to get delegation for priests outside certain parts of Latin America. The fact that it was not given for the benefit of children seriously ill, and approaching death without confirmation, seems to indicate a practical impossibility of getting the faculty for priests to confirm in Europe, or where similar conditions exist.

However, the unnamed commentator in the *Periodica* is not discouraged. He says: "We do not yet give up hope for a reformation of this kind," that is, of the delegation of some priests

[79] "Instructio pro Sacerdote . . .", *AAS* XXVII (1935), 12 *in fine*.
[80] *Loc. cit.*
[81] *Apollinaris*, VIII (1935), 42.
[82] XXIV (1935), 30.

everywhere to confirm children who are dangerously ill.[83] These may well be the words of Vermeersch, for in the *Epitome* he grieves over the number of children who die without confirmation; and he wonders what can be done to give them all an opportunity of being confirmed before death. He asked: "Why is it not possible in places where there are few bishops to give deans and archpriests the faculty of confirming children in danger of death." Then he concludes: "Those who are in authority must determine the opportuneness of this measure; as for us, it is permissible to desire its adoption." [84]

It looks probable that the desire of Vermeersch may some day be realized, notwithstanding the severity of the present discipline. When the Sacred Congregation for the Discipline of the Sacraments met in 1924 to consider the requests which had come from European bishops to have the faculties of Latin American ordinaries extended to them, the eminent Fathers formulated their *dubium* in a significant form: "Is the practice of delegating priests to confirm to be observed within the same limits in future, or for grave and urgent reasons may it be extended in particular cases to Europe also." [85] In spite of the decided negative answer that was rendered the very form of this question indicates that the *very strict* reservation of confirmation to bishops is based on the *practice* of the Holy See. And this practice in turn is based on expediency.[86]

It is more than conceivable, then, that at some future time the Holy See may deem it opportune to give a limited number of priests in all countries the faculty of confirming children and adults in danger of death. The Holy See's desire to have these children confirmed is revealed in the case of the faculty given to ordinaries in China.[87] Why then may there not eventually be a general extension of the favor already granted for the benefit

[83] *Periodica,* XXIV (1935), 30.
[84] *Epitome,* II, n. 66.
[85] *AAS,* XXVII (1935), 14.
[86] Cf. Pallottini, s.v. *"Sacramentum Confimationis,"* nn. 22-23.
[87] Cf. *Primum Concilium Sinense,* n. 273.

of Chinese children? The next division of this article will perhaps reveal some of the possibilities or probabilities in this regard.

The Instruction of 1934 asserts that in giving delegation for confirmation to priests it has always been the mind and serious concern of the Church to provide as far as possible that the priests should possess some ecclesiastical dignity. In the diocese they should enjoy, for example, the rights to use pontificals, and other honorary privileges and insignia, which usually belong to protonotaries apostolic.[88] By the use of distinctive ecclesiastical insignia the extraordinary minister should bear an external likeness to a bishop.[89]

The reason for this is given by the Instruction. It is because it has ever been the maternal care of the Church to prevent any diminution of the reverence due to the sacrament, to obviate occasion for scandal or disappointment, and to have confirmation administered with all the dignity and solemnity that can be employed in the case of a substitute-minister.[90]

There is another important condition to be fulfilled when the priest administers confirmation: he must explain to the people in the vernacular that the bishop alone is the ordinary minister of confirmation; and he must announce that he is confirming only by apostolic indult.[91] The reason for this is to prevent an error on the people's part regarding the minister or ministers of confirmation.[92]

The emphasis which the Holy See puts on the observance of these conditions when a priest administers confirmation, and particularly the reasons given for their careful observance, show the difficulty with which the Holy See is often confronted, when it is asked for faculties for priests to confirm. Even when the request is for urgent emergency cases, for instance, to administer

[88] *AAS*, XXVII (1935), 13.

[89] *Periodica*, XXIV (1935), 30.

[90] *AAS*, XXVII (1935), 13; cf. *Periodica*, XXIV (1935), 30; *Clergy Review*, X (1935), 63; *Homiletic and Pastoral Review*, XXXV (1935), 735.

[91] *AAS*, XXVII (1935), 19.

[92] Pallottini, s.v. "*Sacramentum Confirmationis*," nn. 22-23.

the sacrament to children in danger of death, it is hard to decide what is the more expedient course to follow. If in consequence of the delegation of priests for this ministry there would ensue a notable decrease in reverence for the sacrament of confirmation, or there would be an occasion for scandal, or the solemnity and gravity proper to the administration would be wanting, then indeed the Holy See might feel obliged to deny a request for the delegation of priests.

With regard to the prospect of the delegation of priests in all countries for the administration of confirmation to children and others in danger of death, it must be observed in the light of the recognized obstacles that, when something is done to diminish these obstacles, and when in the changed conditions the relative advantages and disadvantages of delegation are duly weighed, the dream of Vermeersch may be realized, and every Catholic child and adult in danger of death may be given this sacramental title to an augmentation of glory.

Article 6.—Penalty for Attempting to Confirm Without Faculty

Canon 2365: *Presbyter qui nec a iure nec ex Romani Pontificis concessione facultatem habens sacramentum confirmationis ministrare ausus fuerit, suspendatur . . .*"

The penalty prescribed for a priest who attempts to confirm without a faculty is a new sanction introduced by the Code. A former law, to which there is reference in the Code's footnote to canon 2365, inflicted suspension *a divinis* only on Ruthenian-Catholic priests who confirmed children of the Latin rite.[93]

The present penal law refers to any Latin priest[94] usurping the faculty of confirming. His attempt to confirm without delegation is of course fruitless.[95]

To become liable to the penalty, which is *ferendae sententiae*,[96]

[93] *Collectanea*, n. 1243.

[94] Cf. canon 1.

[95] Cf. Chap. IV, Art. 3.

[96] Coronata, *Institutiones Iuris Canonici* (5 vols., Taurini: Marietti, Vol.

it is not sufficient to perform just any part of the confirmation ceremonial. It must be the essential part [97] of the sacramental rite.[98] To be subject to the penalty it is required also that there be not the slightest diminution of imputability on the part of the priest.[99]

The clause "He shall be suspended," is used without any limitation. Therefore it is to be a general suspension in the sense of canon 2279.[100] Nor is the application of the penalty to be left entirely to the discretion of the judges or superior, for the canon uses a preceptive term (*suspendatur*), which indicates that ordinarily the punishment is to be inflicted.[101]

Does a priest attempting to confirm without the faculty also incur an irregularity arising from crime? Few commentators deal with the question: but Cappello [102] and Blat [103] say the irregularity is incurred.

According to canon 985, § 7, men are irregular from crime who, when not ordained to major orders, perform an act of orders reserved to clerics in major orders. By way of commentary on this canon, Cappello writes that the irregularity arises from one's usurpation of a sacred order that one has not received.[104] Augustine too regards the delict as the attempt to perform the act of a higher order than one has received, when that act is reserved to a cleric in sacred orders.[105] Vermeersch-Creusen agree with

III, 1933; Vol. IV, 1935; Vol. V, 1936; Vol. I-II, 2. ed., 1939), Vol. IV, n. 2076; Chelodi-Dalpiza, *Ius Poenale* (4. ed., Tridenti: Liberia Moderna Editrice A. Ardesi, 1935), n. 89.

97 Cf. canon 780.

98 Cf. Blat, *Commentarium,* Lib. V, n. 207; Vermeersch-Creusen, *Epitome,* II, n. 257.

99 Cf. canon 2229, § 2; Coronata, *Institutiones,* IV, n. 2075; Augustine, *Commentary,* VIII, 431.

100 Cf. Coronata, *Institutiones,* IV, n. 2076.

101 Canon 2223, § 3; cf. Blat, *Commentarium,* Lib. V, n. 207.

102 *De Sacramentis,* Vol. II, Pars III, n. 509.

103 *Commentarium,* Vol. III, Pars I, n. 352.

104 *De Sacramentis,* Vol. II, Pars III, n. 509.

105 *Commentary,* IV, 495.

this.[106] In fact, there can be scarcely any dispute about the general meaning of canon 985, § 7.

But its applicability to a priest attempting to confirm without the necessary faculty does not seem beyond the realm of doubt. It has been already noted that the consensus of opinion supports the view that a priest, given the requisite delegation, confirms in virtue of his sacerdotal order.[107] Now, if a priest when confirming acts in virtue of his priesthood, how can it be said that, when in defect of the faculty he attempts to confirm, he is usurping an act of a higher order? And if he is not assuming an act of a higher order than he possesses, how can he be subject to the irregularity mentioned in canon 985, § 7?

Article 7.—Priests to Whom the Law Gives the Faculty To Confirm

Canon 782, § 3: *Hac facultate ipso iure gaudent, praeter S.R.E. Cardinales ad normam can* 239, § 1, *n.* 23, *Abbas vel Praelatus nullius, Vicarius et Praefectus Apostolicus, qui tamen ea valide uti nequeunt, nisi intra fines sui territorii et durante munere tantum.*

The Cardinals of the Holy Roman Church, though they are not necessarily bishops,[108] possess the highest dignity under the Roman Pontiff.[109] In accordance with their exalted position they enjoy everywhere more numerous and more important privileges than any other ecclesiastic except the Holy Father.[110] It is therefore eminently fitting and becoming the Cardinal's dignity that the Supreme Pontiff has endowed them with the faculty of administering confirmation.[111]

The Cardinal's faculty of confirming is not limited by the same conditions as are placed on the faculty of the abbot *nullius* and

[106] *Epitome,* II, n. 257.
[107] Cf. Chap. IV, Art. 3.
[108] Cf. canon 239, § 1, 20°.
[109] Cf. Coronata, *Institutiones,* Vol. I, n. 321.
[110] Cf. canon 239.
[111] Cf. Blat, *Commentarium,* Vol. III, Pars I, n. 79.

others, for in the text cited above Cardinals are distinguished from the others in that no limitation [112] is placed on them.[113] They may administer confirmation in any part of the world, even without the permission of the local ordinary.[114] The only condition that the law imposes is that the confirmation be duly recorded.[115] But the Cardinal is not required to do this personally. If the pastor of those confirmed is present at the ceremony, it is his duty without receiving any admonition to make the prescribed entry in the registers.[116] When the pastor has not been present as the confirmation of his subjects, the Cardinal is required to inform him, or see that he is informed about the confirmation.[117]

As the faculty of confirming is given to the Cardinal because of his dignity, he is not legally obliged as Cardinal to make use of it.[118] Circumstances may occur where he would be obliged in charity to administer confirmation.[119]

Abbots and prelates *nullius* rule their own territories, and are immediately subject to the Roman Pontiff. They have ordinary jurisdiction in the external forum over the clergy and lay people in their respective territories.[120] Within their abbacies and prelacies they enjoy many important privileges.[121]

In such a position the privilege of administering confirmation is not merely a becoming ornament, but a faculty of great practical utility. With the least possible dependence on neighboring bishops in the matter of conferring confirmation they are able to minister to the spiritual needs of their subjects in their own territories.

[112] Cf. canon 239, § 1, 23°.

[113] Cf. Blat, *Commentarium*, Vol. III, Pars I, n. 76; Augustine, *Commentary*, IV, 101.

[114] Cf. *Periodica*, XII (1923), (140).

[115] Canon 239, § 1, 23°.

[116] Canon 798.

[117] Canon 799.

[118] Cf. canon 69; Blat, *Commentarium*, Vol. III, Pars I, n. 79.

[119] Cf. Coronata, *Institutiones*, I, n. 99.

[120] Cf. Coronata, *Institutiones*, I, n. 385.

[121] Cf. canons 323, 325.

The opportuneness and appropriateness of giving abbots and prelates *nullius* the faculty of confirming was realized long before the Code. In several instances they were authorized to confirm.[122] But then the power was given by indult. It is only since the Code that abbots and prelates *nullius* derive their power to confirm from the common law.

The faculty which is given them by the Code can be validly exercised only during the abbot's or prelate's tenure of office, and within their respective jurisdictions. That ruling of course would not apply, when either has received episcopal consecration.[123] In their proper territories they may confirm subjects of other ordinaries under the conditions in which residential bishops confirm non-subjects.[124]

What has been previously written regarding the bishop's obligation to administer confirmation, or have it administered applies also to the abbots and prelates *nullius*.[125] In case of grave negligence on their part the ruling of canon 274, 4°, may be applied.[126]

Though they be only priests of the Latin rite, no special restriction is imposed regarding the rite of the people they can or may confirm.[127] Their faculty is however definitely restricted in its use to the territory of the abbacy or prelacy *nullius*.

The sources contain an interesting case in which an abbot *nullius* strove to obtain the faculty of confirming in the neighboring dioceses, alleging that his predecessor had exercised the faculty outside the abbacy, and that the people would be scandalized by its withdrawal. The response was a decided negative.[128] The Holy See is not disposed to give abbots and prelates *nullius* a wider power.

[122] Cf. S.C. Ep. et Reg., *Nullius Montis Virginis*, 30 mart. 1855—*Fontes*, n. 1972; Benedictus XIV, *De Synodo Dioecesana*, Lib. VII, cap. 7, n. 6.

[123] Cf. Canon 323.

[124] Cf. Augustine, *Commentary*, IV, 102.

[125] Canon 785, § 2.

[126] Cf. Blat, *Commentarium*, Vol. III, Pars I, n. 79.

[127] Cf. Vermeersch-Creusen, *Epitome*, II, n. 62.

[128] S.C.C., *Nullius Caven.*, 11 dec. 1897—*Fontes*, n. 4305.

Should they *presume* to transgress the limits of the faculty conceded to them by law, they are *eo ipso* deprived of that faculty.[129]

Vicars and prefects apostolic are ecclesiastics appointed to rule quasi-dioceses, or ecclesiastical territories where Catholics are few and where it is as yet impossible or impracticable to establish the ordinary diocesan system of administration.[130] The vicar apostolic presides over a territory which is usually more developed than that governed by the prefect apostolic,[131] but even the vicar apostolic is not necessarily a bishop.[132] It is evident that the office of these ecclesiastics demands the enjoyment of extensive faculties, one of the most important of which is the power to administer confirmation. In the exercise of the faculty of confirming they are governed by the same rules as those previously cited and explained for abbots and prelates *nullius*.

The pro-vicar and pro-prefect have no power to confirm while the vicar and prefect are in office and unimpeded.[133] Under the pre-Code law it was certain that they had no power to confirm even during a vacancy of the vicariate or prefecture apostolic.[134] Augustine says that the old ruling still obtains.[135]

It seems that Augustine is mistaken. The Code states that the pro-vicar, pro-prefect or other priest who, in accordance with canon 390, takes charge when the office of vicar or prefect is vacant or impeded, acquires *all* the ordinary and delegated faculties that are attached to the office.[136] Amongst these faculties is the power to administer confirmation. Therefore the priest on whom the administration of the vicariate or prefecture tem-

[129] Canon 2365: " . . . si vero [presbyter] facultatis sibi factae limites praetergredi praesumpserit, eadem facultate eo ipso privatus existat."

[130] Cf. Coronata, *Institutiones*, I, n. 371.

[131] Coronata, *Institutiones*, I, n. 372.

[132] Vermeersch-Creusen, *Epitome*, I, n. 402.

[133] Canon 309, § 2.

[134] *Collectanea*, n. 766; Woywod, *Commentary*, I, 364.

[135] *Rights and Duties of Ordinaries*, p. 221.

[136] Canon 310, § 2.

porarily devolves, must obtain amongst other faculties that of administering confirmation. There is no explicit mention of this in canon 782, § 2; but in the canon the enumeration of clerics who have the faculty by common law is not at all necessarily meant to be explicit in its completeness. Besides, when by canon 310, § 2, in its specific collation with canon 294, the Code very definitely demarcates the powers of the pro-vicar, the pro-prefect and the senior priest who assumes control during the vacancy under the circumstances contemplated in canon 309, it appears altogether unwarranted to gainsay the latter's faculty to administer confirmation, simply because they are not included by name in canon 782, § 3.[137] Augustine's opinion therefore seems to be without a basis.

Though the Code does not mention the Apostolic Nuncio's and Delegate's right to confirm, it seems fitting to give it a brief treatment in this article. They have a right as bishops to administer confirmation in any part of the territory subject to their jurisdiction. They may also confirm on the voyage to and from the place of their assignment.[138] Likewise, when they happen to stop at port for two or three days, they may administer confirmation, for these brief stops are considered a part of the voyage.[139]

In none of these cases are they required to obtain the permission of any local ordinary.[140] But, unless the pastor of those confirmed had been present at the ceremony, the Nuncio or Delegate must either personally or through someone else transmit to him the information required for the parish registers.[141]

Article 8.—Latin Priest's Faculty Given By Indult

Canon 782, § 4: Presbyter latini ritus cui, vi indulti, haec facultas competit, confirmationem valide confert solis fidelibus sui ritus, nisi in indulto aliud expresse cautum fuerit.

[137] Cf. Blat, *Commentarium,* Vol. III, Pars I, n. 76; Vromant, *Commentaria in Formulam Tertiam,* p. 28; Woywod, *Commentary,* I, 364.

[138] "Facultatum quae post Codicem Legatis Apostolicis concedi consueverunt breve commentarium," *Periodica,* XII (1923), (140).

[139] *Periodica,* XII (1923), (140); cf. canon 883.

[140] *Periodica,* XII (1923), (140).

[141] Canon 799.

Under the pre-Code law a Latin priest who was given the faculty of confirming in a certain territory was directed to abstain from confirming orientals in that place.[142] When Orientals were present in the locality, he was required to send detailed information to the Holy See, in order that special provision could be made for them, when necessary.[143] Before the Code law it was not stated whether a Latin priest who confirmed Orientals contrary to the Holy See's instruction acted validly or invalidly.[144]

At the present time a Latin priest who confirms by indult cannot validly confirm Orientals, unless the indult expressly provides for that effect. The faculty given by indult is therefore usually more restricted than that given by common law.[145]

An indult is a particular faculty or favor given by the legislator, usually in the form of a rescript.[146] The indult by which a Latin priest is delegated to confirm may come directly from the Holy See, or from the priest's immediate ordinary. In either of these cases, unless express provision be made to the contrary, the priest can confirm only the people of his own rite.[147]

In view of the general rule that a Latin priest receives a faculty restricted to Latin subjects, the delegating authority who wants to give him a more extended faculty must make the extension to Orientals clear and express. It goes without saying that the delegating authority, familiar with the afore-mentioned rule, will make his intention very evident when he desires to give delegation also for the confirmation of Orientals.

Priests who confirm in view of an indult, like those who confirm by common law, lose their faculty of confirming *eo ipso,* when they *presume* to transgress its limits.[148] Limits may be affixed regarding persons, or places, or both.

[142] Instr. S.C. de Prop. Fide, 4 Maii 1774—*Collectanea,* n. 503.
[143] *Loc. cit.*
[144] Augustine, *Commentary,* IV, 103.
[145] Cf. Vermeersch-Creusen, *Epitome,* II, n. 62.
[146] Cf. Cicognani, *Canon Law,* p. 477.
[147] Cf. Blat, *Commentarium,* Vol. III, Pars I, n. 76.
[148] Canon 2365.

Article 9.—Oriental Priests Not To Confirm Children Of Latin Rite

Canon 782 § 5: *Nefas est presbyteris ritus orientalis, qui facultate vel privilegio gaudent confirmationem una cum baptismo infantibus sui ritus conferendi, eandem ministrare infantibus latini ritus.*

Amongst the Oriental Catholics, with the exception of the Maronites, confirmation is usually administered to children by a simple priest immediately after their baptism.[149] When adults are to be confirmed, or when for some reason confirmation has not been administered along with baptism, it is generally the bishop who confirms.[150]

There is no doubt that oriental priests possess their faculty of confirming through a concession of the Holy See.[151] They enjoy that power in all places except those with reference to which it has been expressly revoked by the Supreme Pontiff.[152] The power has been expressly withdrawn from the Oriental priests in the Island of Cyprus, from those of Bulgaria, and from those of the Maronite division.[153]

Though the Supreme Pontiffs have always had a scrupulous regard for legitimate Eastern customs,[154] they have been equally insistant that Orientals should not impose their practices upon Latins. Time and again therefore have they forbidden Eastern priests, who have the faculty of confirming children of their own rite immediately after baptism, to administer confirmation to children of the Latin rite.[155] Over a long period of time the pro-

[149] Cappello, *De Sacramentis,* Vol. I, *Appendix de iure Ecclesiae Orientalis,* n. 842.

[150] Cappello, *loc. cit.*

[151] Benedictus XIV, *De Synodo Dioecesana,* Lib. VII, cap. 9, n. 3, ff.

[152] Vermeersch, "Casus," *Periodica,* XVI (1927), 120*.

[153] Vermeersch, *loc. cit.*

[154] Cf. Sandalgi, "The Popes and the Christian East," *ER,* LXXXVII (1932), 41-54.

[155] *"Se i sacerdoti orientali autorizzati ad amministrare il baptesimo ai*

hibition was repeated with increasing severity.[156] Oriental bishops were reminded of their grave personal duty to see to it that their priests observed this ruling.[157] The Ruthenian Catholic priests were ordered not to dare administer confirmation to Latin children under penalty of suspension *a divinis ipso facto,* and other *ferendae sententiae* penalties at the discretion of their ordinaries.[158]

In spite of the frequency and severity of the prohibitions, in no case was it indicated that priests contravening the law would be acting invalidly. Never was there evidence of anything more than a prohibition. But naturally questions arose regarding the validity of confirmation which Oriental priests administered to Latins in violation of the severely-worded law.

The Holy See was asked if confirmation administered to Latin children by Greek schismatic priests [159] and to Latin children by Greek uniate priests [160] was to be considered valid, or if it was to be repeated at least *sub conditione.* In every case the answer was that it is not expedient to repeat confirmation, unless there is question of a person to be promoted to tonsure and minor orders, or unless the person himself or his parents ask for confirmation.[161]

bambini di rito latino, possano contemporaneamente amministrare loro anche la cresima?

Negative et ad mentem: Mens est quod cum saepe et gravissime id a S. Sede vetitum sit, moneantur Episcopi orientales ut et ipsi sacerdotes suos ab huiusmodi administratione omnino prohibita deterreant." S.C. de Propaganda Fide, 18 iul. 1886—*Collectanea,* n. 1660.

[156] In the *Collectanea,* n. 552, there is contained a prohibition of the Holy Office issued in 1782.

[157] S.C. de Prop. Fide, 5 iul. 1886—*Collectanea,* n. 1660.

[158] Decr. S.C. de Prop. Fide, 6 oct. 1863: " . . . *Sacerdos vero rutheno-Catholici proli ad latinum ritum spectanti sacramentum baptismi in iisdem commemoratis casibus administrantes, etiam confirmationis sacramentum conferre nullatenus audeant, sub poena suspensionis a divinis ipso facto incurrendae, salvis aliis poenis arbitrio Ordinarii infligendis.*"—*Collectanea,* n. 1243.

[159] S.C.S. Officii, *Jerosolym,* 14 ian. 1885—*Collectanea,* n. 1630.

[160] S.C. de Prop. Fide, 5 iul. 1886—*Collectanea,* n. 1660.

[161] Litt. S.C.S. Off., 16 mar. 1872—*Collectanea,* n. 1381; S.C.S. Off., 2

From the responses this much is certain, namely, that confirmation administered to Latin subjects by Oriental priests, when the faculty of confirming had not been expressly withdrawn from them,[162] was not necessarily invalid. It was at least probably valid.

What basis there was for doubt about the validity of confirmation in the cases that have come up is uncertain. There may have been a question whether the faculty of confirming had been withdrawn from the Eastern priests of certain localities, or whether the faculty of confirming had even been conceded to the priests of a particular territory.[163]

It has not been demonstrated that the reason for doubt about the validity of confirmation administered to Latin children by Oriental priests inhered in any disputable question whether the Holy See had restrained Oriental priests from confirming Latin subjects under penalty of acting invalidly. From the cases that have arisen it certainly cannot be inferred that the Oriental priest's faculty of confirming was in its use restricted *under penalty of invalidity* to Oriental subjects. There were several probable reasons for doubt about the validity of Confirmation in the cases submitted to the Holy See. Hence no one could say with conviction that the validity depended on whether or not the Oriental priests were capable of confirming people of the Latin rite.

The Code has made no change of ruling regarding the Oriental priests' faculty of confirming. The responses given by the Holy See regarding certain doubtful cases therefore retain their force.[164]

Because of the many severe laws that had been issued against Eastern priests confirming children of the Latin rite,[165] it is in-

apr. 1879—*Collectanea,* n. 1515; S.C.S. Officii, *Jerosolym,* 14 ian. 1885—*Collectanea,* n. 1630; S.C. de Prop. Fide, 5 iul. 1886—*Collectanea,* n. 1660.

[162] Cf. *Periodica,* XVI (1927), 177* ff.

[163] Cf. Periodica, *loc. cit.*

[164] Cf. Cappello, *De Sacramentis,* I, n. 206.

[165] Cf. *supra, footnotes,* nn. 155-158.

telligible why the Legislator chose a particularly strong term, *nefas,* to reiterate, or indicate the continuation of, the strict old discipline in this matter. It would be hard, however, to sustain the opinion of Blat that the canon disqualifies Oriental priests from ministering confirmation validly in the supposed circumstances.

He asserts that Oriental priests have no power to confirm people of the Latin rite. That, he thinks, is the force of the word *nefas.*[166] According to this view *nefas* denotes not merely what may not but also what cannot be done.

But if one takes the word *nefas* in itself one can hardly agree that it has the force attributed to it by Blat. While it is admittedly a strong term, it does not of itself denote lack of what may be called physical power. Though *nefas* is used in canon 817 to prohibit the consecration of bread without wine, or vice versa, and to prohibit the consecration of both outside the celebration of Mass, it is commonly held that the consecration of one element without the other, or the consecration of both outside Mass, is possible.[167]

For other very good internal reasons this term cannot be taken in the sense in which it is accepted by Blat. In its general norms, the Code lays down, amongst other principles, the rule that *only* those laws which *expressly* or *equivalently* say that an act is invalid or that a person is incapable are to be regarded as nullifying or as disqualifying if the requirement of law is contravened.[168]

In whatever manner paragraph 5 of canon 782 is understood, its import cannot amount to more than a mere prohibition, however severe it may be.[169] The reading of canon 782, § 5, may be rendered: it is not allowed, it is definitely forbidden, it is most strictly prohibited; but by no legitimate translation or paraphrase can the canon be construed to mean that an Oriental priest, who has the faculty of confirming children of his own rite, is *incapable* of confirming children of the Latin rite. In fact, according to the

[166] *Commentarium,* Vol. III, Pars I, n. 76.
[167] Cf. Noldin-Schmitt, *Summa,* III, n. 103.
[168] Canon 11.
[169] Cf. Augustine, *Commentary,* IV, 104.

principle of interpretation set forth in canon 11, it must be concluded that the import of paragraph 5 of canon 782 is merely prohibitive and not disqualifying in its potential juridical effect. It does not assert either equivalently or expressly that an Oriental priest cannot validly confirm children of the Latin rite. Therefore, unless the rule of canon 11 is arbitrarily ignored, the law under discussion must be understood in its sole character of a prohibitory law.

That there is question only of lawfulness seems to be apparent also from the context. The previous paragraph had said that a priest of the Latin rite who enjoys the faculty of confirming by indult can *validly* confirm *only* people of his own rite, unless other express provision is made in the indult. Now, it seems altogether improbable that the Legislator, who had in one paragraph so clearly indicated the invalidity of confirmation administered to Orientals by a Latin priest, should in the very next paragraph but vaguely imply that confirmation administered to Latins by an Oriental priest is invalid. If one paragraph reads: Latin priests *can validly confirm only* children of their own rite, unless it is expressly provided otherwise in their indult, and the very next paragraph reads: *it is forbidden,* or *it is prohibited sub gravi* that an Oriental priest confirm children of the Latin rite, then obviously the latter paragraph cannot have the force of the former.

Whether the paragraph under discussion be considered in itself and in relation to the preceding paragraph, or whether it be considered in relation to canon 11, it seems certain that an Oriental priest with the faculty or privilege of confirming Oriental children is merely forbidden to confirm children of the Latin rite, but that he is not incapable of confirming them.

Practically all authorities are in favor of the opinion that the Oriental priest in question certainly, or, at the least, in all probability has the essential power to confirm children of the Latin rite.[170]

[170] Vermeersch, *Theologia Moralis,* III, n. 243; Cappello, *Periodica,* XVI (1927), 130; Prümmer, *Manuale Iuris Canonici,* p. 377; Aertnys-Damen, *Theologia Moralis,* II, n. 87; Augustine, *Commentary,* IV, 104; Woywod,

Regarding the severity of the present law, there is no doubt that it would be gravely illegal and sinful for an Oriental Priest to confirm children of the Latin rite.[171] This is apparent from the word *nefas,* as well as from the rigidity of the former law.[172]

Greek-Ruthenian priests moreover are subject to the penalty of suspension, when they confirm children of the Latin rite.[173] But that is particular law.[174]

An Oriental priest who is restrained from confirming children of the Latin rite is not forbidden to confirm children of an Oriental rite different from his own, provided that in the other rite priests are accustomed to confirm at the time of baptism.[175] Thus Syrian, Coptic, Ruthenian, Chaldean and Malabar priests may confirm children of any of their several rites,[176] but none of these priests may confirm children of the Maronite rite. The reason is that amongst the Maronites the bishop alone administers confirmation,[177] while amongst the people of these other Eastern rites the priest usually confirms.[178] In view of particular Oriental law, however, the general rule enunciated in the first sentence of this paragraph may need some qualification.

A question of local importance calls for some consideration here. There used to be some doubt about the Ruthenian-Greek priests' power to confirm in the United States.[179] The apostolic letter *"Ea semper"* [180] had expressly denied them the power. A

Commentary, I, 263; O'Donnell, "Confirmation in the New Code," *IER* (5th series), XI (1918), 210.

171 Cappello, *Periodica,* XVI (1927), 130*; Augustine, *Commentary,* IV, 104.

172 Cf. *supra,* footnotes nn.

173 Cf. Augustine, *Commentary,* IV, 104; S.C. de Prop. Fide, 5 iul. 1886—*Collectanea,* n. 1660.

174 *Collectanea, loc. cit.*

175 S.C.S. Off., 22 apr. 1896—*Collectanea,* n. 1926; cf. Augustine, *Commentary,* IV, 115.

176 Cappello, *De Sacramentis,* I, nn. 844 ff.

177 Cappello, *op. cit.,* I, n. 844.

178 Cf. Cappello, *ibidem,* n. 842 ff.

179 Cf. Augustine, *Commentary,* IV, 104-105.

180 14 iun. 1907—*ASS,* XLI (1908), 7; cf. Augustine, *loc. cit.*

subsequent decree [181] which might have denoted a total rearrangement,[182] of the status of Orientals in the United States, said nothing about this particular point. Therefore the uncertainty. Perplexed with this problem, Duskie communicated with the Ordinary for the Greek-Ruthenians from Galicia in the United States, and received the information that the restriction of the Apostolic letter *Ea semper* had been revoked; and consequently the Ruthenian-Greek priests now validly and lawfully confirm children of their own rite in the United States.[183]

Article 10.—Use of Local Privilege of Confirming

Canon 784: *Presbytero quoque licet, si apostolico locali privilegio sit munitus, in designato sibi territorio confirmare etiam extraneos, nisi ipsorum Ordinarii expresse vetuerint.*

A local privilege is a privilege which has been granted directly to a *place* and only indirectly to a person attached to, or exercising a function in, that place.[184] A priest's local privilege of confirming therefore is conceded for the practical benefit of a locality,[185] and not, like that given a Cardinal, for the adornment or enhancement of his personal dignity.[186]

Relative to the priest enjoying such a privilege the Legislator has considered it advisable to grant the permission of confirming outsiders too, provided that the outsiders' ordinary has not expressly objected. Outsiders, or strangers, are those who are under the jurisdiction of an ordinary other than the one ruling the territory where the priest confirms.[187]

This is the same limited freedom which a bishop has to con-

[181] S.C. de Prop. Fide pro Negotiis Ritus Orientalis, decr. "*Cum Episcopo,*" 17 aug. 1914—*AAS,* VI (1914), 458-463.

[182] Cf. canon 22.

[183] *The Canonical Status of Orientals in the United States,* The Catholic University of America, Canon Law Studies, n. 48 (Washington, D. C.: The Catholic University of America, 1928), p. 95, footnote 28.

[184] Cf. Coronata, *Institutiones,* I, n. 87.

[185] Cf. canon 782, § 2.

[186] Cf. Blat, *Commentarium,* III, Pars I, n. 77.

[187] Cf. Blat, *Commentarium,* Vol. III, Pars I, n. 77.

firm strangers coming into his diocese.[188] The commentary given on canon 783, § 1 [189] is therefore, in the main, applicable to canon 784, for canon 784 is but an extension of the concession of canon 783, § 1, to abbcts and prelates *nullius*, vicars and prefects apostolic, and other priests having the local apostolic privilege of administering confirmation.

There may however be special reason which would justify a bishop in opposing the confirmation of his subjects by a priest. For instance, there may be danger that his subjects would lose their esteem for confirmation, should they receive it from a priest.[190]

Whatever the bishop's or ordinary's reason for not permitting his people to be confirmed by a priest having the faculty, the administration would be valid, if, notwithstanding the prohibition, the priest confirmed, for the bishop cannot impose an invalidating limitation on the faculty given a priest by the Holy See.[191]

But, if it is a case of a Latin priest having a local *indult* to confirm Latins only, it is very important to remember the ruling of canon 782, § 4, which affects not only the lawful but likewise the valid exercise of his faculty.

When a priest confirms strangers it is important also that he keep in mind the necessity which he may be under to notify the proper pastor, so that the administration of confirmation may be duly recorded.[192]

The historical background and further commentary on this article can be found in Chapter III, Article 3.

Article 11.—The Priest's Obligation To Confirm

Canon 785, § 2: *Eadem obligatio confirmandi tenetur presbyter, privilegio apostolico donatus, erga illos quorum in favorem est concessa facultas.*

[188] Canon 783, § 1.
[189] Cf. Chap. III, Art. 3.
[190] Cf. *AAS*, XXVII (1935), 13.
[191] Cf. Blat, *Commentarium*, Vol. III, Pars I, n. 78; canon 11.
[192] Canon 799.

The residential bishop's obligation to confirm has already been discussed. Since that obligation is the same as the one resting on a priest who, in the interests of certain people, has been given the faculty of confirming,[194] it follows that what has been written[195] on the residential bishop's obligation to confirm (or have confirmation administered) is also true of this priest's obligation. There is no need here for repetition.

In some cases there will be a difference between the source of the obligation of confirming which rests upon a bishop and the source of the same obligation resting on a priest. The bishop has an obligation to confirm *ex officio,* while a priest with a local *indult* may be obligated not *ex officio,* but by positive law.[196]

The Church uses the same method of enforcing the obligation of confirming, whether it binds a priest or a bishop: the metropolitan should report grave negligence in this matter to the Holy See.[197]

Finally, what has been stated regarding offerings on the occasion of confirmation,[198] evidently holds, whether confirmation be administered by a priest or by a bishop.

[194] Cf. *AAS,* XXVII (1935), 17.

[195] Cf. Chap. III, Art. 5.

[196] Cf. Blat, *Commentarium,* Vol. III, Pars I, n. 79.

[197] Canon 785, § 4; cf. *supra,* p.

[198] Cf. Chap. III, Art. 8.

CONCLUSIONS

The principal conclusions that may be drawn from the preceding study are:

1. that in his episcopal consecration a bishop became ordinary minister of confirmation either by the reception of a distinct sacrament, or by the extension of the priestly character;

2. that no bishop can be deprived of his power to administer confirmation;

3. that heretical and schismatical ministers *as such* are not incapable of administering confirmation;

4. that the opinion which holds that a bishop could *ex natura rei* delegate priests to administer confirmation is scarcely tenable;

5. that canon 209 is not applicable to the faculty of confirming or of delegating for confirmation;

6. that the error of prominent Scholastics regarding the possibility of a simple priest being delegated to confirm was founded on a forged decretal;

7. that a grave reason has always been required, and is still necessary, before the Church will give a priest authority to administer confirmation;

8. that the Oriental custom whereby priests normally confirm is not in actual conflict with the Code's doctrine on the ordinary and extraordinary ministers[1] or with Western usage;

9. that there is no essential reason why the Holy See will not eventually delegate many priests to administer confirmation to infants and adults in danger of death;

10. (a) that no certain precedent can be adduced to show that a priest can be delegated to bless chrism, and (b) that he very probably cannot be given this delegation;

11. that the quality which a priest receives in his faculty to confirm is, according to the best modern opinion, a *peculiar dignity* essential to the minister of confirmation;

12. that the consensus of canonical opinion favors the view that

[1] Canon 782, §§ 1, 2.

Oriental priests with the privilege or faculty of confirming children of their own rite are not "incapable" of confirming Latin subjects;

13. that the law gives pro-prefects and pro-vicars the faculty of confirming when they assume temporary administration of the prefecture or vicariate in the circumstances contemplated in canon 409 § 1;

14. that a priest does not become irregular when he attempts to confirm without the necessary delegation;

15. that a bishop and duly delegated priest in like position have an obligation to confirm a dying person requesting this sacrament, unless the effort necessary to administer it in a given case is proportionately too great;

16. that the minister of confirmation may derive a right from provincial law or legitimate custom to accept offerings for his services.

BIOGRAPHICAL NOTE

John Jerome Coleman was born in Gurteen, Co. Sligo, Ireland, May 12, 1906. He received his elementary education at a local National School; and his secondary education at the Salesian High School and College, London England. His major seminary course was taken at St. Patrick's Ecclesiastical College, Carlow, Ireland, where he was ordained in June, 1934. The four subsequent years he spent in parish work in the Diocese of Spokane. In September, 1938 he entered the school of Canon Law at the Catholic University of America, from which he received the degree of Baccalaureate in Canon Law in June, 1939, and the degree of Licentiate in Canon Law in June, 1940.

BIBLIOGRAPHY

Sources

Acta Apostolicae Sedis, Commentarium Officiale, Romae, 1909—.

Acta Sanctae Sedis, 41 vols., Romae, 1865-1908.

Acta et Decreta Concilii Plenarii, Baltimorensi Secuundi (1866), Baltimorae, 1894.

Acta et Decreta Concilii Plenarii, Baltimorensi Tertii (1884), Baltimorae, 1886.

Canones et Decreta Sacrosancti Oecumenici Concilii Tridentini, Romae, 1882.

Codex Iuuris Canonici, Pii X Pontificis Maximi jussa digestus Benedicti Papae XV auctoritate promulgatus, Romae, Typis Polyglottis Vaticanis, 1918.

Codicis Iuris Canonici Fontes, cura Emi Petri Card. Gasparri editi, 9 vols., Romae (Later, Civitate Vaticana) Typis Polyglottis Vaticanis, 1923-1939. (Vols. VII, VIII, IX ed. cura et studio Emi. Justiniani Card. Seredi).

Collectanea S. Congregationis de Propaganda Fide, 2 vols., Romae, Typographia Polyglotta S.C. de Propaganda Fide, 1907.

Corpus Iuris Canonicis, editio Lipsiensis II (Richter-Friedberg) 2 vols., Lipsiae, 1922.

Corpus Scriptorum Ecclesiasticorum Latinorum, editum consilio et impensis Academiae Litterarum Caesariae Vindobonae (Corpus Vindobonense), 68 vols., 1866—.

Decreta Authentica Congregationis Sacrorum Rituum, 6 vols., Romae, 1898-1927.

Denzinger, Henr. et Umberg, Joh. B., *Enchiridion Symbolorum Definitionum et Declarationum,* ed. 21-23, Friburgi Brisgoviae: Herder, 1937.

Harduin, Jean, *Conciliorum Collectio Regia Maxima,* 12 vols., Parisiis, 1715.

Juris Ecclesiastici Graecorum Historia et Monumenta, Jussu Pii IX Pont. Max. Curante J. B. Cardinal Pitra, Romae, 1864.

Pallottini, S., *Collectio Omnium Conclusionum, et Resolutionum Quae in causis propositis apud Sacram Congregationem Cardinalium S. Concilii Tridentini interpretum Prodierunt ab eius institutione anno MDLXIV ad MDCCCLX, distinctis titulis alphabetico ordine per materias digestas,* 18 vols., Romae, 1868-1895.

Primum Concilium Sinense, Anno 1924 . : . *Celebratum*: *Acta-Decreta et Normae—Vota etc.,* Zi-Ka-Wei: Typographia Missionis Catholicae (T'OU-SÊ-WÊ), 1929.

Mansi, Joannes, *Sanctorum Conciliorum Nova et Amplissima Collectio,* 53 vols., Parisiis, 1901-1927.

Migne, Jacques Paul, *Patrologiae Cursus Completus, Series Graeca,* 161 vols., Parisiis, 1856-1868.

——————*Patrologiae Cursus Completus, Series Latina,* 221 vols., Parisiis, 1844-1864.

Thesaurus Resolutionum Sacrae Congregationis Concilii, 167 vols., Romae, 1718-1908.

Reference Works

Aertnys, J.—Damen, C., *Theologia Moralis Secundum S. Alfonsum de Ligorio,* 11. ed., 2 vols., Taurinorum Augustae: Marietti, 1928.

Augustine, C., *Rights and Duties of Ordinaries,* St. Louis: Herder Book Company, 1924.

Ayrinhac, H. A., *Legislation on the Sacraments in the New Code of Canon Law,* New York: Longmans Green and Co., 1928.

(Bachofen), Charles Augustine, *A Commentary on the New Code of Canon Law,* 4. ed., 8 vols., St. Louis: B. Herder, 1921-1929.

Ballerini-Palmieri, *Opus Theologicum Morale,* 14. ed., 7 vols., Prati, 1889-1893.

Barbosa, A., *Iuris Ecclesiastici Universi Libri Tres,* Lugduni, 1656.

Bellarminus, Robertus Franciscus, *Opera Omnia,* 12 vols., Parisiis, 1870-1874.

Benedict XIV, *De Synodo Dioecesana,* 2 vols., Romae, 1806.

Bevilacoua, Americo, *De Episcopi seu Ordinarii ex Novo Codice Canonico Iuribus et Obligationibus,* Romae: Pustet, 1921.

Billot, Ludivicus, *De Ecclesiae Sacramentis,* 4. ed., 2 vols., Romae, 1906.

Bingham, Joseph, *The Antiquities of the Christian Church,* 2 vols., London, 1856.

Blat, Albertus, *Commentarium Textus Codicis Canonici,* 6 vols., Romae: Collegio "Angelico," 1921-1927.

Bouix, D., *Tractatus de Episcopo,* 2 vols., Parisiis, 1859.

Bouscaren, T. Lincoln, *Canon Law Digest,* 2 vols., Milwaukee: The Bruce Publishing Co., 1934 and 1937.

Cappello, Felix M., *Tractatus Canonico-Moralis de Sacramentis,* 3 vols., Vol. I, II, 3. ed., Taurinorum Augustae: Marietti, 1938, Vol. III, 4. ed., Taurinorum Augustae: Marietti, 1939.

Catholic Encyclopedia, The, 16 vols., and 2 suppls., New York, 1907-1922.

Chardon, C., *Histoire des Sacraments,* 6 vols., Parisiis, 1745.

Chase, Frederic Henry, *Confirmation in the Apostolic Age,* London, 1913.

Chelodi-Dalpias, *Ius Poenale,* 4. ed., Tridentini: Liberia Moderna Editrice A. Ardesi, 1935.

Cicognani, Amleto, *Canon Law,* authorized English version, by J. O'Hara and F. Brennan, Philadelphia: Dolphin Press, 1934.

Conte Matthaeus A. Coronata, *Institutiones Iuris Canonici,* 5 vols., (Vols. I et II, 2 ed.,) Taurini: Marietti, 1933-1939.

D'Ales, Adhemar, *De Baptismo et Confirmatione,* Paris: Gabriel Beauchesne, 1927.

De Augustinis, Aemilius, *De Re Sacramentaria,* 2. ed., 3 vols., Romae, 1889.

Dens, Petrus, *Tractatus de Sacramentis in Genere et de Sacramentis Baptismi et Confirmationis in Specie,* Mechlinae, 1860.

Dictionnaire D'Archéologie Cretiénne et De Liturgie, 14 vols., Paris: Letouzey et Ane, 1924—.

Dictionnaire de Theologie Catholique, 25 vols., Paris: Letouzey et Ane, 1903-1937.

Diehl, Wilhelm, *Zur Geschichte der Konfirmation,* Giessen: J. Ricker, 1897.

Duskie, John A., *The Canonical Status of the Orientals in the United States,* The Catholic University of America, Canon Law Studies, n. 48, Washington, D. C.: The Catholic University of America, 1928.

Estius, Guilielmus, *In Quattuor Libros Sententiarum Commentaria,* 2 vols., Parisiis, 1696.

Eusebius, *The Ecclesiastical History of Eusebius Pamphilius* (Translated from the Greek by C. F. Cruse), London, 1879.

Ferraris, F. Lucius, *Prompta Biblotheca, Canonica, Juridica, Moralis, Theologica, nec non Ascetica, Polemica, Rubricistica, Historica,* ed. Migne, 8 vols., Parisiis, 1860-1863.

Ferreres, J. B., *Compendium Theologiae Moralis,* 14 ed., 3 vols., Romae: Eugenius Surbirana, 1928.

Fortesque, Adrian, *The Uniate Eastern Churches,* New York: Benziger Bros., 1923.

Genicot, Eduardus, *Theologiae Moralis Institutiones,* 2 vols., Lovanii, 1897.

Genicot, E., et Salsmans, I., *Institutiones Theologiae Moralis,* II. ed., 2 vols., Bruxellis: Dewit, 1927.

Gury-Ballerini, *Compendium Theologiae Moralis,* 17. ed., 2 vols., Romae, 1866.

Hall, A.C.A., *Confirmation,* London, 1912.

Hinschius, R., *System des katholischen Kirchenrechts mit besonderer Ruecksicht auf Deutschland,* 6 vols., Berlin, 1869-1897.

Hunteman, Ulricus, *Bullarium Franciscanum,* Florentiae, Typ: Coll. S. Bonaventura, 1929.

Kenrick, F. P., *Theologia Moralis,* 3 vols., Baltimorae, 1886.

——————*A Treatise on Baptism and Confirmation,* Baltimore, 1852.

Kilker, Adrian J., *Extreme Unction,* The Catholic University of America, Canon Law Studies, n. 32, Washington, D. C.: The Catholic University of America, 1926.

Konings, Antonius, *Theologia Moralis,* 5. ed., 2 vols., Neo Eboraci, 1882.

Labouche, L., *The Three Sacraments of Initiation,* New York: Benzinger, 1922.

La Croix, C., *Theologia Moralis,* 3 vols., Coloniae, 1719.

Lahouse, Gustave, *Tractatus de Sacramentis in Genere, De Baptismo, De Confirmatione et De Eucharistia,* Brugis, 1902.

Layman, P., *Theologia Moralis,* 2 vols., Patavii, 1733.

Lehmkuhl, Augustinus, *Theologia Moralis,* 2 vols., 10. ed., Friburgi Brisgoviae, 1902.

Lucidi, Angelus, *De Visitatione Sacrorum Liminum,* 3. ed., 2 vols., Romae, 1883.

Marc, Cl., Gestermann, F. X., et Raus, J. B., *Institutiones Morales Alphonsianae,* 19. ed., 2 vols., Lugduni: Vitte, 1933.

Marca, Petrus de, *De Concordida Sacerdotii et Imperii,* Bambergae, 1788.

Martene, Edmundus, *De Antiquis Ecclesiae Ritibus,* 3 vols., Rotomagi, 1700.

Merkelbach, Benedictus H., *Summa Theologiae Moralis ad Mentem D. Thomae et ad Norman Iuris Novi,* 2. ed., 3 vols., Parisiis: Typis Desclée, De Brouwer et Soc., 1935-1939.

Miaskiewicz, Francis J., *Supplied Jurisdiction According to Canon* 209, The Catholic University of America, Canon Law Studies, n. 122, Washington, D. C.: The Catholic University of America, 1940.

Noldin, H., Schmitt, A., *Summa Theologiae Moralis,* 20. ed., Oeniponte: Rauch, 1929.

Noort, G. Van., *Tractatus de Sacramentis in Genere, Baptismo, Confirmatione et SS. Eucharistia,* Amstelodami, 1910.

O'Dwyre, Michael, *Confirmation, A Dogmatic Thesis for Degree of Doctor,* New York, 1915.

Pallavicino, Sfortia, *Vera Concilii Tridentini Historia,* 3 vols., Antverpiae, 1670.

Pesch, Christianus, *Praelectiones Dogmaticae,* 11 vols., Friburgi Brisgoviae, 1896.

Poulet-Raemers, *Church History,* 2. ed., 2 vols., London: Herder, 1936.

Prümmer, Dominicus M., *Manuale Iuris Canonici,* 4. et 5. ed., Friburgi Brisgoviae: Herder, 1927.

——————*Manuale Theologiae Moralis secundum Principia S. Thomae Aquinatis,* 4. et 5. ed., 3 vols., Friburgi Brisgoviae: Herder, 1928.

Sabetti, A., Barrett. T., *Compendium Theologiae Moralis,* 34. ed., Neo-Eboraci: Pustet, 1939.

Saintebeuve, Hieronymi de, *Tractatus de Sacramento Confirmationis,* Lovanii, 1778.

Schmalzgrueber, Franciscus, *Ius Ecclesiasticum Universum,* 12 vols., Romae, 1843-1845.

Sipos, Stephanus, *Enchiridion Iuris Canonici,* Pecs, 1926.

Suarez, Franciscus, *Opera Omnia,* 26 vols., Parisiis, 1856-1861.

Tanquerey, Ad., *Synopsis Theologiae Dogmaticae,* Parisiis, Decleé et Socii, 1937.

Thesaurus Theologicus, 13 vols., Venetiis, 1762-1763.

Thomassinus, Ludovicus, *Vetus et Nova Ecccleslae Disciplina,* 3 vols., Venetiis, 1730.

Tournelly, Horatius, *Tractatus de Universa Theologia Morali,* Parisiis, 1750.

Trombelli, Joannes, C., *Tractatus de Sacramentis,* 2 vols., Bononiae, 1775.

Van Espen, Zegerus B., *Scripta Omnia,* 4 vols., Lovanii, 1753.

Van Noort, G., *Tractatus de Sacramentis,* Amstelodami, 1910.

Vermeersch, A., *Theologiae Moralis Principia Responsa, Consilia,* 2. ed., 3 vols., Brugis: Firme Charles Beyaert, 1926-1927.

Vermeersch, A., Creusen, J., *Epitome Iuris Canonici,* 3 vols., Mechliniae: H. Dessain, Vol. I, 5. ed., 1934: Vol. II, 5. ed., 1936; Vol III, 6. ed., 1937.

Villien, A., *History and Liturgy of the Sacraments* (English Translation by Edwards), London: Burns Oates, 1932.

Vromant, G., *Facultates Apostolicae Quas Sacra Congregatio de Propaganda Fide Delegare Solet Ordinariis Missionum, Commentaria in Formulam Tertiam,* Lovain: Museum Lessianum, 1926.

Wernz, F.—Vidal, P., *Ius Canonicum,* 8 vols., Romae: Apud Aedes Universitatis Gregorianiae, 1923-1938.

Wigman, Theodore, *The Doctrine of Confirmation,* New York, 1897.

Woywod, Stanislaus, *A Practical Commentary on the Code of Canon Law,* 4. ed., 2 vols., New York: Wagner, 1932.

Articles

Cappello, F., "Ius Ecclesiae Latinae cum Iure Ecclesiae Orientalis Comparatum," *Jus Pontificum,* VII (1927), 55-71.

Connell, F., "The Episcopate," *ER,* LXXII (1925), 335-345.

Deslandes, J., "Le Pretre Oriental Ministre de la Confirmation," *Echos D'Orient,* XXIX (1930), 5-15.

Gasquet, J., "The Early History of Baptism and Confirmation," *The Dublin Review,* 4. S. (1895), 136-147.

McDonald, W., "The Sacrament of Extreme Unction," *ITQ,* II (1907), 330-345.

Roberts, C., "Episcopate and Presbyterate," *ACR,* IX (1932), 316-331.

Sandalgi, P., "The Popes and the Christian East," *ER,* LXXXVII (1932), 41-54.

Souarn, R., "De Presbytero Orientali Confirmationis Ministro," *Jus Pontificium,* XI (1931), 133-143.

Tromp, S., "Actio Catholica in Corpore Christi," *Periodica,* XXV (1936), 1-38.

Umberg, J., "Confirmatione Baptismus Perficitur," *Ephemerides Theologicae Lovanienses,* I (1924), 505-517.

Zerba, C., "Instructio pro Simplici Sacerdote Sacramentum Confirmationis ex Sedis Apostolicae Delegatione Administrante,"*Apollinaris,* VIII (1935), 41-46.

Periodicals

Apollinaris, Romae, 1928—

Australasian Catholic Record, The, Manly, 1923—

Clergy Review, The, London, 1931—

Dublin Review, The, Dublin, 1836—

Ecclesiastical Review, The (originally *The American Ecclesiastical Review*), Philadelphia, 1889—

Échos d'Orient, Paris.

Ephemerides Theologicae Lovanienses, Brugis, 1924—

Irish Ecclesiastical Record, The, Dublin, 1864—

Irish Theological Quarterly, The, Dublin, 1906—

Jus Pontificium, Romae, 1921—

Monitore Ecclesiastico, Il, Romae, 1879—

Nouvelle Revue Theologique, Paris, 1869—

Perfice Manus, Torino, 1926—

Periodica de Re Canonica et Morali utili Praesertim Religiosis et Clericis, Bruges, 1905—

Revue Bénedictine, Lille et Bruges, 1884—

Theologisch-praktische Quartalschrift, Linz, 1832—

Zeitschrift für katholische Theologie, Innsbruck, 1876—

Abbreviations

AAS—Acta Apostolicae Sedis.

ACR—Australasian Catholic Record, The.

AER—American Ecclesiastical Review.

ASS—Acta Sanctae Sedis.

Collectanea—Collectanea S.C. de Propaganda Fide.

CSEL—Corpus Scriptorum Ecclesiasticorum Latinorum.

Fontes—Codicis Iuris Canonici Fontes cura . . . Gasparri editi.

Harduin—Conciliorum Collectio Regia Maxima.

Mansi—Sanctorum Conciliorum Nova et Amplissima Collectio.
MPG—Patrologiae Cursus Completus, series Graeca.
MPL—Patrologiae Cursus Completus, series Latina.
NRT—Nouvelle Revue Théologique.
Thesaurus—Thesaurus Resolutionum S.C.C.

ALPHABETICAL INDEX

CANON LAW STUDIES

1. Freriks, Rev. Celestine A., C.PP.S., J.C.D., Religious Congregations in Their External Relations, 121 pp., 1916.
2. Galliher, Rev. Daniel M., O.P., J.C.D., Canonical Elections, 117 pp., 1917.
3. Borkowski, Rev. Aurelius L., O.F.M., J.C.D., De Confraternitatibus Ecclesiasticis, 136 pp., 1918.
4. Castillo, Rev. Cayo, J.C.D., Disertacion Historico-Canonica sobre la Potestad del Cabildo en Sede Vacante o Impedida del Vicario Capitular, 99 pp., 1919 (1918).
5. Kubelbeck, Rev. William J., S.T.B., J.C.D., The Sacred Pentitentiaria and Its Relations to Faculties of Ordinaries and Priests, 129 pp., 1918.
6. Petrovits, Rev. Joseph J.C., S.T.D., J.C.D., The New Church Law On Matrimony, X-461 pp., 1919.
7. Hickey, Rev. John J., S.T.B., J.C.D., Irregularities and Simple Impediments in the New Code of Canon Law, 100 pp., 120.
8. Klekotka, Rev. Peter J., S.T.B., J.C.D., Diocesan Consultors, 179 pp., 1920.
9. Wanenmacher, Rev. Francis, J.C.D., The Evidence in Ecclesiastical Procedure Affecting the Marriage Bond, 1920 (Printed 1935).
10. Golden, Rev. Henry Francis, J.C.D., Parochial Benefices in the New Code, IV-119 pp., 1921 (Printed 1925).
11. Koudelka, Rev. Charles J., J.C.D., Pastors, Their Rights and Duties According to the New Code of Canon Law, 211 pp., 1921.
12. Melo, Rev. Antonius, O.F.M., J.C.D., De Exemptione Regularium, X-188 pp., 1921.
13. Schaaf, Rev. Valentine Theodore, O.F.M., S.T.B., J.C.D., The Cloister, X-180 pp., 1921.
14. Burke, Rev. Thomas Joseph, S.T.D., J.C.D., Competence in Ecclesiastical Tribunals, IV-117 pp., 1922.
15. Leech, Rev. George Leo, J.C.D., A Comparative Study of the Constitution, "Apostolicae Sedis" and the "Codex Juris Canonici," 179 pp., 1922.
16. Motry, Rev. Hubert Louis, S.T.D., J.C.D., Diocesan Faculties According to the Code of Canon Law, II-167 pp., 1922.
17. Murphy, Rev. George Lawrence, J.C.D., Delinquencies and Penalties in the Administration and Reception of the Sacraments, IV-121 pp., 1923.
18. O'Reilly, Rev. John Anthony, S.T.B., J.C.D., Ecclesiastical Sepulture in the New Code of Canon Law, II-129 pp., 1923.

19. Michalicka, Rev. Wenceslas Cyrill, O.S.B., J.C.D., Judicial Procedure in Dismissal of Clerical Exempt Religious, 107 pp., 1923.
20. Dargin, Rev. Edward Vincent, S.T.B., J.C.D., Reserved Cases According to the Code of Canon Law, IV-103, pp., 1924.
21. Godfrey, Rev. John A., S.T.B., J.C.D., The Right of Patronage According to the Code of Canon Law, 153 pp., 1924.
22. Hagedorn, Rev. Francis Edward, J.C.D., General Legislation on Indulgences, II-154 pp., 1924.
23. King, Rev. James Ignatius, J.C.D., The Administration of the Sacraments to Dying Non-Catholics, V-141 pp., 1924.
24. Winslow, Rev. Francis Joseph, A.F.M., J.C.D., Vicars and Prefects Apostolic, IV-149 pp., 1924.
25. Correa, Rev. Jose Servelion, S.T.L., J.C.D., La Potestad Legislativa de la Iglesia Catolica, IV-127 pp., 1925.
26. Dugan, Rev. Henry Francis, A.M., J.C.D., The Judiciary Department of the Diocesan Curia, 87 pp., 1925.
27. Keller, Rev. Charles Frederick, S.T.B., J.C.D., Mass Stipends, 167 pp., 1925.
28. Paschang, Rev. John Linus, J.C.D., The Sacramentals According to the Code of Canon Law, 129 pp., 1925.
29. Pointek, Rev. Cyrillus, O.F.M., S.T.B., J.C.D., De Indulto Exclaustrationis necnon Saecularizationis, XIII-289 pp., 1925.
30. Kearney, Rev. Richard Joseph, S.T.B., J.C.D., Sponsors at Baptism According to the Code of Canon Law, IV-127 pp., 1925.
31. Bartlett, Rev. Chester Joseph, A.M., LL.B., J.C.D., The Tenure of Parochial Property in the United States of America, V-108 pp., 1926.
32. Kilker, Rev. Adrian Jerome, J.C.D., Extreme Unction, V-425 pp., 1926.
33. McCormick, Rev. Robert Emmett, J.C.D., Confessors of Religious, VIII-266 pp., 1926.
34. Miller, Rev. Newton Thomas. J.C.D., Founded Masses According to the Code of Canon Law, VII-93 pp., 1926.
35. Roelker, Rev. Edward G., S.T.D., J.C.D., Principles of Privilege According to the Code of Canon Law, XI-166 pp., 1926.
36. Bakalarczyk, Rev. Richardus, M.I.C., J.U.D., De Novitiatu, VIII-208 pp., 1927.
37. Pizzuti, Rev. Lawrence, O.F.M., J.U.L., De Parochis Religiosis, 1927. (Not printed).
38. Bliley, Rev. Nicholas Martin, O.S.B., J.C.D., Altars According to the Code of Canon Law, XIX-132 pp., 1927.
39. Brown, Mr. Brendan Francis, A.B. LL.M., J.U.D., The Canonical Juristic Personality with Special Reference to Its Status in the United States of America, V-212 pp., 1927.

40. Cavanaugh, Rev. William Thomas, C.P., J.U.D., The Reservation of the Blessed Sacrament, VIII-101 pp., 1927.
41. Doheny, Rev. William J., C.S.C., A.B., J.U.D., Church Property: Modes of Acquisition, X-118 pp., 1927.
42. Feldhaus, Rev. Aloysius H., C.PP.S., J.C.D., Oratories, IX-141 pp., 1927.
43. Kelly, Rev. James Patrick, A.B., J.C.D., The Jurisdiction of the Simple Confessor, X-208 pp., 1927.
44. Neuberger, Rev. Nicholas J., J.C.D., Canon 6 or the Relation of the Codex Juris Canonici to the Preceding Legislation, V-95 pp., 1927.
45. O'Keefe, Rev. Gerald Michael, J.C.D., Matrimonial Dispensations, Powers of Bishops, Priests and Confessors, VIII-232 pp., 1927.
46. Quigley, Rev. Joseph A.M., A.B., J.C.B., Condemned Societies, 139 pp., 1927.
47. Zaplotnik, Rev. Johannes Leo, J.C.D., De Vicariis Foraneis, X-142 pp., 1927.
48. Duskie, Rev. John Aloysius, A.B., J.C.D., The Canonical Status of the Orientals in the United States, VIII-196 pp., 1928.
49. Hyland, Rev. Francis Edward, J.C.D., Excommunication, Its Nature, Historical Development and Effects, VIII-181 pp., 1928.
50. Reinmann, Rev. Gerald Joseph, O.M.C., J.C.D., The Third Order Secular of Saint Francis, 201 pp., 1928.
51. Schenk, Rev. Francis J., J.C.D., The Matrimonial Impediments of Mixed Religion and Disparity of Cult, XVI-318 pp., 1929.
52. Coady, Rev. John Joseph, S.T.D., J.U.D., A.M., The Appointment of Pastors, VIII-150 pp., 1929.
53. Kay, Rev. Thomas Henry, J.C.D., Competence in Matrimonial Procedure, VIII-164 pp., 1929.
54. Turner, Rev. Sidney Joseph, C.P., J.U.D., The Vow of Poverty, XLIX-217 pp., 1929.
55. Kearney, Rev. Raymond, A., A.B., S.T.D., J.C.D., The Principles, of Delegation, VII-149 pp., 1929.
56. Conran, Rev. Edward James, A.B., J.C.D., The Interdict, V-163 pp., 1930.
57. O'Neil, Rev. William H., J.C.D., Papal Rescripts of Favor, VII-218 pp., 1930.
58. Bastnagel, Rev. Clement Vincent, J.U.D., The Appointment of Parochial Adjutants and Assistants, XV-257 pp., 1930.
59. Ferry, Rev. William A., A.B., J.C.D., Stole Fees, V-135 pp., 1930.
60. Costello, Rev. John Michael, A.B., J.C.D., Domicile and Quasi-domicile, VII-201 pp., 1930.
61. Kremer, Rev. Michael Nicholas, A.B., S.T.B., J.C.D., Church Support in the United States, VI-1930.

62. Angulo, Rev. Luis, C.M., J.C.D., Legislation de la Iglesia sobre la intencion en la application de la Santa Misa, VII-104 pp., 1931.
63. Frey, Rev. Wolfgang Norbert, O.S.B., A.B., J.C.D., The Act of Religious Profession, VIII-174 pp., 1931.
64. Roberts, Rev. James Brendan, A.B., J.C.D., The Banns of Marriage, XIV-140 pp., 1931.
65. Ryder, Rev. Raymond Aloysius, A.B., J.C.D., Simony, IX-151 pp., 1931.
66. Campagna, Rev. Angelo, Ph.D., J.U.D., Il Vicario Generale del Vescovo, VII-205 pp., 1931.
67. Cox, Rev. Joseph Godfrey, A.B., J.C.D., The Administration ot Seminaries, VI-124 pp., 1931.
68. Gregory, Rev. Donald J., J.U.D., The Pauline Privilege, XV-165 pp., 1931.
69. Donohue, Rev. John F., J.C.D., The Impediment of Crime, VII-110 pp., 1931.
70. Dooley, Rev. Eugene A., O.M.I., J.C.D., Church Law On Sacred Relics, IX-143 pp., 1931.
71. Orth, Rev. Raymond Clement, O.M.C., J.C.D., The Approbation of Religious Institutes, 171 pp., 1931.
72. Pernicone, Rev. Joseph M., A.B., J.C.D., The Ecclesiastical Prohibition of Books, XII-267 pp., 1932.
73. Clinton, Rev. Connell, A.B., J.C.D., The Paschal Precept, IX-108 pp., 1932.
74. Donnelly, Rev. Francis B., A.M., S.T.L., J.C.D., The Diocesan Synod, VIII-125 pp., 1932.
75. Torrente, Rev. Camilo, C.M.F., J.C.D., Las Processiones Sagradas, V-145 pp., 1932.
76. Murphy, Rev. Edwin J., C.PP.S., J.C.D., Suspension Ex Informata Conscientia, XI-122, pp., 1932.
77. Mackenzie, Rev. Eric F., A.M., S.T.L., J.C.D., The Delict of Heresy in its Commission Penalization, Absolution, VII-124 pp., 1932.
78. Lyons Rev. Avitus E., S.T.B., J.C.D., The Collegiate Tribunal of First Instance, XI-147 pp., 1932.
79. Connolly, Rev. Thomas A., J.C.D., Appeals, XI-195 pp., 1932.
80. Sangmeister, Rev. Joseph V., A.B., J.C.D., Force and Fear as Precluding Matrimonial Consent, V-211 pp., 1932.
81. Jaeger, Rev. Leo A., A.B., J.C.D., The Administration of Vacant and Quasi-vacant Episcopal Sees in the United States, IX-229 pp., 1932.
82. Rimlinger, Rev. Herbert T., J.C.D., Error Invalidating Matrimonial Consent, VII-79 pp., 1932.
83. Barrett, Rev. John D.M., S.S., J.C.D., A Comparative Study of the Third Plenary Council of Baltimore and the Code, IX-221 pp., 1932.

84. Carberry, Rev. John J., Ph.D., S.T.D., J.C.D., The Juridical Form of Marriage, X-177 pp., 1934.
85. Dolan, Rev. John L., A.B., J.C.D., The Defensor Vinculi, XII-157 pp., 1934.
86. Hannan, Rev. Jerome D., A.M., S.T.D., LL.B., J.C.D., The Canon Law of Wills, IX-517 pp., 1934.
87. Lemieux, Rev. Delisle A., A.M., J.C.D., The Sentence in Ecclesiastical Procedure, IX-131 pp., 1934.
88. O'Rourke, Rev. James J., A.B., J.C.D., Parish Registers, VII-109 pp., 1934.
89. Timlin, Rev. Bartholomew, O.F.M., A.M., J.C.D., Conditional Matrimonial Consent, X-381 pp., 1934.
90. Wahl, Rev. Francis X., A.B., J.C.D., The Matrimonial Impediments of Consanguinity and Affinity, VI-125 pp., 1934.
91. White, Rev. Robert J., A.B., LL.B., S.T.B., J.C.D., Canonical Ante-Nuptial Promises and the Civil Law, VI-152 pp., 1934.
92. Herrera, Rev. Antonio Parra, O.C.D., J.C.D., Legislation Ecclesiastica sobra el Ayuno y la Abstinencia, XI-191 pp., 1935.
93. Kennedy, Rev. Edwin J., J.C.D., The Special Matrimonial Process in Cases of Evident Nullity, X-165 pp., 1935.
94. Manning, Rev. John J., A.B., J.C.D., Presumption of Law in Matrimonial Procedure, XI-111 pp., 1935.
95. Moeder, Rev. John M., J.C.D., The Proper Bishop for Ordination and Dismissorial Letters, VII-135 pp., 1935.
96. O'Mara, Rev. William A., A.B., J.C.D., Canonical Causes For Matrimonial Dispensations, IX-155 pp., 1935.
97. Reilly, Rev. Peter, J.C.D., Residence of Pastors, IX-81 pp., 1935.
98. Smith, Rev. Mariner T., O.P., S.T.L., J.C.D., The Penal Law For Religious, VII-169 pp., 1935.
99. Whalen, Rev. Donald W., A.M., J.C.D., The Value of Testimonial Evidence in Matrimonial Procedure, XIII-297 pp., 1935.
100. Cleary, Rev. Joseph F., J.C.D., Canonical Limitations on the Alienation of Church Property, VIII-141 pp., 1936.
101. Glynn, Rev. John C., J.C.D., The Promoter of Justice, XX-337 pp., 1936.
102. Brennan, Rev. James H., S.S., A.M., S.T.B., J.C.D., The Simple Convalidation of Marriage, VI-135 pp, 1937.
103. Brunini, Rev. Joseph Bernard, J.C.D., The Clerical Obligations of Canons, 139 and 142, X-121 pp., 1937.
104. Connor, Rev. Maurice, A.B., J.C.D., The Administrative Removal of Pastors, VIII-159 pp., 1937.
105. Guilfoyle, Rev. Merlin Joseph, J.C.D., Custom, XI-144 pp., 1937.
106. Hughes, Rev. James Austin, A.B., A.M., J.C.D., Witnesses in Criminal Trials of Clerics, IX-140 pp., 1937.

107. Jansen, Rev. Raymond J., A.B., S.T.L., J.C.D., Canonical Provisions for Catechetical Instruction, VII-153 pp., 1937.
108. Kealy, Rev. John James, A.B., J.C.D,, The Introductory Libellus in Church Court Procedure, XI-121 pp., 1937.
109. McManus, Rev. James Edward, C.SS.R., J.C.D., The Administration of Temporal Goods in Religious Institutes, XVI-196 pp., 1937.
110. Moriarity, Rev. Eugene James, J.C.D., Oaths in Ecclesiastical Courts, X-115 pp., 1937.
111. Rainer, Rev. Eligius George, C.SS.R., J.C.D., Suspension of Clerics, XVII-249 pp., 1937.
112. Reilly, Rev. Thomas F., C.SS.R., J.C.D., Visitation of Religious, VI-195 pp., 1938.
113. Moriarty, Rev. Francis E., C.SS.R., J.C.D., The Extraordinary Absolution from Censures, XV-334 pp., 1938.
114. Connolly, Rev. Nicholas P., J.C.D., The Canonical Erection of Parishes, X-132 pp., 1938.
115. Donovan, Rev. James Joseph, J.C.D., The Pastor's Obligation in Prenuptial Investigation, XII-322 pp., 1938.
116. Harrigan, Rev. Robert J., M.A., S.T.B., J.C.D., The Radical Sanation of Invalid Marriages, VIII-208 pp., 1938.
117. Boffa, Rev. Conrad Humbert, J.C.D., Canonical Provisions for Catholic Schools, X-211 pp., 1939.
118. Parsons, Rev. Anscar John, O.M. Cap., J.C.D., Canonical Elections, XII-236 pp., 1939.
119. Reilly, Rev. Edward Michael, A.B., J.C.D., The General Norms of Dispensation, X-156 pp., 1939.
120. Ryan, Rev. Gerald Aloysius, A.B., J.C.D., Principles of Episcopal Jurisdiction, XII-172 pp., 1939.
121. Burton, Rev. Francis James, C.S.C., A.B., J.C.D., A Commentary on Canon 1125, X-222 pp., 1940.
122. Miaskiewicz, Rev. Francis Sigismund, J.C.D., Supplied Jurisdiction according to Canon 209, XII-340 pp., 1940.
123. Rice, Rev. Patrick William, A.B., J.C.D., Proof of Death in Prenuptial Investigation, VIII-156 pp., 1940.
124. Anglin, Rev. Thomas Francis. M.S., J.C.L., The Eucharistic Fast.
125. Coleman, Rev. John Jerome, J.C.L., The Minister of Confirmation.
126. Downs, Rev. John Emmanuel, A.B., J.C.L., The Concept of Clerical Immunity.
127. Esswein, Rev. Anthony Albert, J.C.L., Extrajudicial Penal Powers of Ecclesiastical Superiors.
128. Farrell, Rev. Benjamin Francis, M.A., S.T.L., J.C.L., The Rights and Duties of the Local Ordinary Regarding Congregations of Women Religious of Pontifical Approval.

129. Feeney, Rev. Thomas John, A.B., S.T.L., J.C.L., Restitutio in Integrum.
130. Findlay, Rev. Stephen William, O.S.B., A.B., J.C.L., Canonical Norms Governing the Deposition and Degradation of Clerics.
131. Goodwine, Rev. John, A.B., S.T.L., J.C.L., The Right of the Church to Acquire Property.
132. Heston, Rev. Edward Louis, C.S.C., Ph.D., S.T.D., J.C.L., The Alienation of Church Property in the United States .
133. Hogan, Rev. James John, S.T.L., J.C.L.,, Judicial Advocates and Procurators.
134. Kealy, Rev. Thomas M., A.B., Litt. B., J.C.L., Dowry of Women Religious.
135. Keene, Rev. Michael James, O.S.B., J.C.L., Religious Ordinaries and Canon 198.
136. Kerin, Rev. Charles A., S.S., M.A., S.T.B., J.C.L., The Privation of Christian Burial.
137. Louis, Rev. William Francis, M.A., J.C.L., Diocesan Archives.
138. McDevitt, Rev. Gilbert Joseph, A.B., J.C.L., Legitimacy and Legitimation.
139. McDonough, Rev. Thomas Joseph, A.B., J.C.L., Apostolic Administrators.
140. Meier, Rev. Carl Anthony, A.B., J.C.L., Penal Administrative Procedure Against Negligent Pastors.
141. Schmidt, Rev. John Rogg, A.B., J.C.L., The Principles of Authentic Interpretation in Canon 17 of the Code of Canon Law.
142. Slafkosky, Rev. Andrew Leonard, A.B., J.C.L., The Canonical Episcopal Visitation of the Diocese.
143. Swoboda, Rev. Innocent Robert, O.F.M., J.C.L., Ignorance in Relation to the Imputability of Delicts.
144. Dubé, Rev. Arthur Joseph, A.B., J.C.L., The General Principles for the Reckoning of Time in Canon Law.
145. McBride, Rev. James T., A.B., J.C.L., Incardination and Excardination of Seculars.

www.ingramcontent.com/pod-product-compliance
Lightning Source LLC
LaVergne TN
LVHW050221080826
844660LV00012B/449

* 9 7 8 0 8 1 3 2 2 3 1 4 8 *